THE WONDER ISLAND BOYS

ADVENTURES ON STRANGE ISLANDS

ROGER THOMPSON FINLAY

1st WORLD
LIBRARY
Literary Society

The Wonder Island Boys: Adventures on Strange Islands

Roger Thompson Finlay

© 1st World Library, 2009
PO Box 2211
Fairfield, IA 52556
www.1stworldlibrary.com
First Edition

LCCN: 2009923509

Softcover ISBN: 978-1-4218-8879-8
Hardcover ISBN: 978-1-4218-8978-8
eBook ISBN: 978-1-4218-8780-7

Purchase *"The Wonder Island Boys: Adventures on Strange Islands"*
as a traditional bound book at:
www.1stWorldLibrary.com/purchase.asp?ISBN=978-1-4218-8879-8

1st World Library is a literary, educational organization
dedicated to:

- Creating a free internet library of downloadable ebooks

- Hosting writing competitions and offering book publishing
scholarships.

1st World Library Literary Society

Giving Back to the World

"If you want to work on the core problem, it's early school literacy."

- James Barksdale, former CEO of Netscape

"No skill is more crucial to the future of a child, or to a democratic and prosperous society, than literacy."

- Los Angeles Times

"Literacy... means far more than learning how to read and write... The aim is to transmit... knowledge and promote social participation."

- UNESCO

"Literacy is not a luxury, it is a right and a responsibility. If our world is to meet the challenges of the twenty-first century we must harness the energy and creativity of all our citizens."

- President Bill Clinton

"Parents should be encouraged to read to their children, and teachers should be equipped with all available techniques for teaching literacy, so the varying needs and capacities of individual kids can be taken into account."

- Hugh Mackay

CONTENTS

CHAPTER I

THE STRANGE OARS AND ROPES

"I am awfully anxious to know where the charted islands can be that John spoke about," remarked George, as Harry was consulting the plans of the boat they were building.

"They must be in this section of the southern seas, or his party wouldn't have sailed in this direction," answered Harry, after a pause.

"Do you think he would be offended if we spoke to him about it!"

"No;" answered Harry, after some reflection. "He has spoken to me about it several times. But why do you ask!"

"For the reason that I think it would be a grand thing to hunt them up."

Harry laughed, and then slowly said: "That would be a big thing to undertake. But what about going home?"

"I hadn't forgotten that. I meant that when we came back it would be proper for us to undertake."

"Well, haven't you had enough trouble during the past two years?" And Harry laughed, just as though they hadn't gone through sufficient trials to last a life time.

"I wouldn't mind going through the same experiences, when I remember what we have learned and what all of us have accomplished," responded George, as he looked through the window, reflectively, and watched the natives at work.

*   *   *   *   *

It will be difficult to understand the force of the above conversation, unless the reader knows the situation in which the boys were placed at the time it took place, and the locality of the scene where the conversation was held.

Over two years previously two boys, George Mayfield and Harry Crandall, were members of a school training ship which left the Harbor of New York, for a cruise in southern waters, the object being to instruct the crew of seventy boys in the art of seamanship, as well as to give them a foundation knowledge in the arts and sciences.

On board they became intimate with a gray-haired Professor, who became very ill. They were particularly attracted to him, and waited upon him, until they reached the Pacific Ocean, where, for some reason the ship met a catastrophe, and the crew were compelled to take to open boats.

The two boys, with several companions, and the Professor, were together in one of the life boats, and after leaving the sinking ship a terrific gale, one of the great monsoons, separated them from the companion boats, and for six days they were driven about in the vast ocean, absolutely helpless. During this time all their young companions were washed overboard, and they were driven to the point of despair, when they were cast ashore on an island.

They were thus placed on an unknown land, with nothing but their scanty clothing, and devoid even of a knife. There is no indication that the land was inhabited, and for the first three months, while recuperating, they had no opportunity to go far from the spot where they landed.

After the Professor had regained his health, they began to make a few necessary things, and hunt for the food which was necessary to preserve life. As they grew bolder, however, they fashioned crude implements, like bows and arrows, and primitive articles of utility.

They made a few trips into the interior, and then saw the first indications which pointed to the presence of inhabitants. From some of the traces it was evident that the people must be savages, and then they saw the necessity of preparing themselves to meet hostile neighbors.

Then began the most remarkable series of adventures on the part of the boys, under the instruction of the Professor, to provide not only the necessaries of life, but many of the luxuries. While engaged in the different enterprises they undertook numerous excursions, all of which confirmed them in the first intimations that they had landed on an island, and that it contained one or more savage tribes.

To recount all that the boys did, even in the briefest space, would be impossible in this book, and it is not necessary, in order to relate the happenings from this time on; but some things are necessary, because we shall have to deal with incidents which took place during their adventures, and this volume also brings into the scene several characters, in addition to the three which have been named, as the principal participants.

The incidents referred to were called by the boys "the mysteries." When they landed on the island they erected a flag pole, and improvised a flag which was kept at half mast, and mounted on a high point, so that it would attract passing ships, if their island chanced to be in the path of vessels. During one of their excursions the flag pole and staff disappeared.

For the purpose of making one of the trips by water a boat was built, and they sailed it up a large stream, only to find that within ten miles of their home was an immense cataract, or falls, around which they could not porter the vessel. It was left below the falls in a secure position, and ten days later, when they went for it, were surprised at its disappearance.

Later on it was found miles away, but the little closets which they had built in to hold their food and clothing, had disappeared, and they were still more startled to find a pair of oars, which they could not have made, attached to the boat.

In repairing the boat a note was discovered, written by some one who could not have been a member of their ill-fated vessel. This added to their perplexities, for it indicated that white people had been on the island, as well as savages.

Then they found strange ropes, evidently fashioned by a crude hand; a skull of a well-developed man was picked up on the shore not far from their home; part of the wreckage of a vessel was discovered; a herd of yaks was captured and a mysterious brand deciphered on one of them.

But in their wanderings they found the entrance to a cavern, and this was explored, resulting in finding that it was formerly a pirates' lair, and they were astounded at finding immense wealth in its hidden recesses.

They industriously searched the island, and found numerous ores which were dug out and smelted and from which they were able to build many things that added to their comfort; and finally, firearms were constructed, and powder made.

They spent much of the time in chemical experiments, in hunting for and gathering the different vegetables, and fibres, and from the latter learned how to weave cloth, to make felt, and to turn skins into leather from the animals which they hunted.

Their adventures were not wholly devoid of the amusing things of life. In one of the expeditions they captured a young Orang-outang. This was carefully taught to do many things, and it became not only a valuable assistant, and a wonderful scout in their wanderings, but it afforded them immense amusement, which was appreciated by the boys.

And now, having been provided with suitable weapons, they determined to go on voyages of discovery, being prompted in this course, because they found in the wreckage along one of the rivers, and far in the interior, a life boat which was a companion to their own which had been lost when they were stranded in the great tempest.

It was evident to them that some of their companions were on the island, and probably, captives. This made the quest a most exciting one, so every energy was bent toward the end of helping the unfortunates.

On the initial expedition, after the completion of the first weapons, they came into contact with several tribes of savages, one of whom was captured, after being wounded. It developed that he was a chief of one of the tribes which at that time were at war with each other.

Returning from this trip they discovered at their home a distinguished looking white man in rags, totally devoid of intellect, and unable to speak. It was evident that he had met with some accident, but he was entirely harmless, and obediently took up and performed every sort of manual labor,—in fact, was an expert in any sort of mechanical operation required of him.

In hunting, or in scouting, he was a perfect specimen of the hunter, or the soldier. It seemed to be an instinct with him to render every kind of service that might be needed, with the gun, or the tools which were all about him. In the absence of a better name they christened him John.

On the second trip into the unknown portions of the island they met three of the savage tribes, with whom they had several battles, and one of the natives was wounded and captured. While wandering through the forests, in their efforts to return to their home, they ran into a savage village, where they were successful in rescuing two boys who had been shipmates on the *Investigator* which went down months before.

While this was a source of joy it was clouded by the information that they were not the ones who came to the island in the life boat that the boys had found in the river. This was evidence that others must still be in the island, and probably held as captives.

Some months after the silent John came to them, his reason and the ability to speak returned to him, and he told a wonderful tale of his wanderings, and that which impressed the boys most was the information that he had shipped in a vessel which was designed to search out the treasures hidden in the islands of the South seas.

From hints which he dropped from time to time, the islands containing the treasure were charted, and later on, one of the caves so charted was found on the island they now occupied, although they also found several which were not alluded to and could not be recognized by the description, according to the story told by John.

John was an educated man, an archaeologist, and, next to the Professor, had the most varied knowledge of any one the boys ever met, and it can be understood, that their association with men of that class made them remarkably active in seeking out and understanding the wonderful things that nature presents in every field of human activity.

In order to be as brief as possible with this part of the story, it is necessary to add that the rescue of the two boys, and the restoration of John's faculties, made a strong party, and new weapons were made, and the real expeditions through the island begun.

During the first extended trip, the Professor was captured. Out of this misadventure grew some of the most remarkable series of events, but finally, they were successful in rescuing four more of their former companions, and two of John's shipwrecked companions.

The capture of the Chief, formerly alluded to, and the subsequent rescue of a chief who was about to be offered up as a sacrifice, served as a means to bring two of the tribes to the rescue of those in the expedition, and the Professor, by his wisdom, was able to enlist the services of the tribe which had captured him.

The events which lead directly up to the beginning of this volume were brought about by the enmity of two of the most bitter and vindictive tribes, which compelled the Professor and the boys to form an expedition against those hostiles, in which four other tribes assisted.

They captured the Chief, and rescued two of their former companions, and then built a town called Unity, where the advantages of civilization were taught the natives, and to which place many of the families of the natives emigrated.

All the chiefs formed an alliance of peace, and the Professor was made the chief magistrate. After peace and order had been restored, the boys again began to long for home. Prior to this they had determined to build a ship large enough to take them to the nearest shipping point, and they were now feverishly engaged in the work with the aid of the natives, who were eager to learn how the white men built the wonderful things which they saw all about them.

It will, therefore, be understood, that the remarks of George, at the opening of this chapter, had reference to the fact that the most important of the islands, or the ones having the most of the treasures could not be the one on which they resided, but pertained to some other localities.

"Well, if there is anything I am interested in, it is to know why the wonderful buildings we found at the Illyas' village were put up at that place, and what caused all trace of them to be lost," said Harry, after George had expressed his last opinion.

"Do you remember what John said, after we came out of the cave below the village?"

"No; what was it!"

"He said the copper in the cave might explain it."

After the capture of the last tribe, John demanded that the Chief inform them of the location of the Hoodoo, or Medicine Men of the tribe, and he reluctantly consented, but the Chief warned them, that to attempt to enter the cave would mean Death.

John knew that the Chief and the people believed the death tales told by the Medicine Men, as it was tales of this kind which enabled them to maintain such a hold on the people. In order to destroy the power of those people, who really had been the cause of much of their troubles, John announced that he would take the Chief and his followers to the cave, and that he would then go into the cave alone, and come out again, to prove that the Medicine Men had lied to him.

John entered the cave, and single-handed captured the Krishnos, as they were called, and brought them out, thus verifying his statement that those men had deceived the people. Soon thereafter John and the boys entered the cave, which, from the description he had, contained an immense amount of treasure, but they were unable to discover any trace of it if it existed.

By accident the calcareous deposit was broken off at one part in their search, and below was found a dark material, which, after examination, was found to be copper. It was not in its native state, but was a product produced by smelting the ore, and they uncovered an immense quantity of it, sufficient to show that the portion of the cave in which it was found was really a storehouse.

Not more than a mile away was the Native village, where they held the tribe captive. The village was absolutely unlike anything else in the form of habitations found in the island. Three of the buildings were large structures, built in three of the well-known types of architecture, and the other parts of the village were laid off regularly.

Surrounding the village was a strong embankment, as though originally used as a fortification, and the village itself was located on the side of a hill, betokening sanitary considerations.

"But I do not see," observed George, "what the copper in the cave had to do with the town?"

"Nor do I," responded Harry. "Suppose we see John at the first opportunity. There are other things besides the copper I would like to know. John has asked every one that he has come into contact with about the different wrecks that have come ashore within the past two years, and no one seems to have any idea that more than two of the *Investigator's* boats came ashore."

"Well, if they did it isn't at all likely that they could come to the southern shore, when the wrecked vessel was to the north of the island."

"It is just for that reason," responded George, "that I believe we shall find other islands in the vicinity, and who knows but some of the boats reached those islands?"

"I am with you," said Harry. "Shall we talk to John about it?"

"By all means. But stop! Why not have a talk with the Professor first?"

"Good idea. We owe everything to him."

CHAPTER II

A MYSTERIOUS MESSAGE

The town of Unity was located about ten miles from the sea, on a little stream, which had a waterfall, from which they derived the power for turning the machinery which had been put up. This consisted of a saw mill, a small foundry, a machine shop, as well as grist mill and other mechanism suitable for a town.

All these enterprises were now being operated by the natives. The leading commercial genius of the town was Blakely, who was one of the owners of the vessel on which John had sailed from San Francisco, and which was also wrecked by the same monsoon which sent the schoolship *Investigator* to the bottom.

It was Blakely's idea that the work of the natives could be profitably turned to raising coffee, cocoa, and the different fibres which naturally grew all over the island, and in order to take advantage of the crops which could be grown there it would be necessary to open communication with the outside world.

To do this meant that they must build a ship, and thus reach civilization, and vessels could then bring such things to the islands as the natives could use, and take away the produce that the natives could turn out.

Such a plan was one which was heartily seconded by all the boys, who, although they had been engaged in the most wonderful experiences, were homesick, and longed to see their parents in the States, and thus relieve them of their anxiety, after an absence of more than two years.

It was with a will that all took a hand in the work, and the ship was nearing completion. They had no facilities for making a large engine, so the vessel was a sailer, with a small propeller, and the largest size engine they could turn out was to be used as an auxiliary.

The next evening while the Professor, John and the boys were together, Harry brought up the subject of the talk of the previous evening.

"George and I have been talking about making a voyage of discovery."

The Professor looked at Harry with that genial smile which the boys had learned to love. Without answering for the moment, the old man turned to John, as the latter's face lit up.

"I thought you boys were homesick?" he said.

"Well, yes," answered George. "But only for a little while."

"Only homesick for a little while?" and the Professor's hearty laugh followed.

"I mean we are homesick,—that is, we can be cured of it in a little while."

Without relaxing that broad smile, the Professor continued: "I suppose you want to be cured before you go on the voyage of discovery? Is that it?"

"Yes."

"But what do you expect to discover!" asked John, gravely.

"Just what you suggested on one occasion," said Harry.

"We want to know where the treasures are on the islands," remarked George.

"Then, there is another thing," ventured Harry. "I don't think all the boats of our ship were lost, and it is likely that they found refuge on some other island."

"But how do you know there are other islands near here?" asked the Professor.

"Well, I don't know, only from what John has said."

John looked at Harry for a moment quizzically, and then said: "When did I say so?" he asked with a smile.

"When you told about the charts of the treasure caves."

"But we have found them, haven't we?"

"Yes; but not all of them."

"That is true; and your argument is correct. Unquestionably, there are other islands, probably not in the immediate vicinity, but near enough that they could have caught some of the boats. I quite agree with you that we ought to make the attempt. The Professor and I have just been talking of taking up the matter in order to relieve any who might have been so unfortunate as to be east away."

"I am surprised," said the Professor, "that you are not through with treasure hunting, and want some more of it."

"But you know, Professor, that some of the most interesting times we had were during the investigations we made at the big cave at the Cataract on Wonder Island!"

"Quite true; but think of the immense riches you now have. In the vault beneath the floor of the main shop you have the combined treasure of the two caves," continued the Professor.

"Yes; and that shall be taken back by you to your homes in the States, and you will want to enjoy it," and John said this with a most sincere air, as he looked at the boys.

"That would be nice," said Harry reflectively. "But if we are there the only thing we can do is to spend it, and there is no particular fun in doing that."

"What? No fun in spending the money?" exclaimed the Professor.

"Why, we haven't spent a cent since we have been here, and we have enjoyed every hour of the time, except—except—" and George hung his head for a moment.

"I know," said the dear old Professor; "I know what you mean. Home still has a warm place in your heart. That is right. You must see your home, and then,—"

"Then we want to come back," broke in Harry.

"It makes me happy to see that the lessons of the past while we have been together has impressed on your minds one thing; that it is not riches which give happiness."

"I know that," said Harry. "When I go out and see these poor people here, and I meet smiles on every face, and a welcome everywhere, the thought that we have tried to make them feel and know that wars were wrong, and that true happiness consists in trying to make others happy, it gives me more pleasure than all the gold which we took from the caves of the Buccaneers."

"Yes, and there is another thing, that I have been thinking about," said George. "I really don't think the people here are so bad, and never have thought so."

"Well, they have been doing some pretty bad things," remarked John. "I would like to know what makes you think as you do."

"I mean, that if it wasn't for certain classes, like the Krishnos, say, the people would not be trying to sacrifice each other. Those fellows are the ones who lie to the people, just as the fellows at the last cave told the people and the Chiefs that if they went into the cave the Great Spirit would destroy them."

John and the Professor both laughed, while the boys looked on. There did not seem to be anything amusing about that, and they wondered why they should laugh at George's remark.

"Did it ever occur to you how like that is to the white man's way of doing things?" asked John.

"I never thought of that!" said Harry.

"Do the white people act that way, too?" inquired George. "I never knew that we had people who tried to deceive others so they could give them up as a sacrifice?"

"What do you think the Krishnos deceive the people for?" asked the Professor.

"So as to give them the power," answered George.

"Quite true. But what is the object of that power?"

"So they can rule?"

"Yes; but what gives them the power to rule?"

"Oh, I see now! They get paid for it! And that is why the Krishnos have all the best things, and are better cared for than even the chiefs are?"

"You have given the right answer. The Krishnos don't want to sacrifice human life because they love to do it, but because in the doing of it they inspire fear, and through fear they can get what they want."

"But, Professor, you haven't yet told us how that is like the white people do it."

"In exactly the same way. The Krishnos own the big gun factories, and they tell the chiefs that the people across the river, or on the other side of the mountain are going to rise up against them, and they must arm the people and attack them. You see the white man's Krishnos have a great cave, called a gun factory, and while he does not want to offer up any sacrifices for the love of it, he does so because it is his business to make guns, and ammunition, and shells which explode with terrific force, and destroy hundreds at every shot."

"Well, after all, we are not much better than the savages here, are we?" said Harry, as he looked around, with a sad expression.

"We have advanced a little beyond them," interpolated John. "We have tried to systematize the killing. The savage goes at it without regard. But the white man has set rules to conduct the slaughter. Of course, the rules do not say that they shall not kill but it does point out the impolite ways of killing."

The Professor smiled at this homely way of putting it, but the boys looked doubtfully at John's exposition, and then George ventured to remark: "I can see the force of it, and it is my opinion that the savage way is, after all, the most reasonable."

"If it is not the most reasonable," answered the Professor, "it is certainly the most logical. But we are getting away from our subject. I understand from what John says that within the next week we shall be able to launch the vessel!"

"Yes," answered Harry. "Everything is now so far ahead that in two weeks more we can be ready to sail."

"That is well. I hear there is considerable rivalry among the men to go with you?"

"But aren't you going with us?" asked George in a voice of alarm.

"No; my place is here. I have no desire to go back. I have induced John, much against his will, I know, to go with you, but I cannot leave my people here. I will welcome you only the more gladly when you return."

Harry was almost in tears, as he said: "But we wanted you to go back with us so we could take you to our homes and let our people see you. They would be so happy to see you and to hear you talk."

"Thank you so much for the kind invitation. Sometime in the future, when everything is properly settled here, and I can see my way clear, I will consider it an honor to visit your homes, and enjoy the friendship of your dear ones; but not now."

The door opened quietly, and Angel stepped in, Angel being the Orang-outang to which we have alluded. He was now nearly as tall as George. He gravely shambled over to the Professor, and placed an envelope in his hand.

Angel was the most wonderful character in that community. He was the pet and the playmate of all the children. No one dared to harm him or offer an insult. Such a thing would have caused an insurrection in that town.

While he could not speak, he could understand practically everything that was told him. Daily he performed many extraordinary tasks, thanks to the training and care that George had bestowed upon him from the day he had become a captive.

The Professor opened the envelope, and adjusted his glasses. As he read his eyes opened wider and wider, while John and the boys drew closer. While reading one of the sheets the Professor was slowly unfolding a scrap of dark colored material, smaller than the sheet he was reading.

"What is it?" asked Harry.

"The letter is from Blakely," he said as he passed the papers to John. "And what do you think it is about?"

All eagerly peered at the letter and then at the brown missive, whatever it was.

"Read it aloud," said the Professor.

John handed it to George, and this is Blakely's letter:

"SOUTH MOUNTAIN,
Below Illya.

"My Dear Professor:

"I felt sure that my view as to the character of the mountain range below the town was correct. Copper outcroppings were found as far south as the range can be seen, and there is also silver in abundance. This will surely be a profitable field for the natives. Yesterday, while prospecting on the southeastern side of the main ridge, I was surprised to find a part of a metal pot, evidently of cast iron. Quite a number of articles, of no particular value were lying near, but within the fragment of the pot, and protected by a shale of rock, was the enclosed scrap, which I thought might interest you, as you have a leaning in the direction of finding out hidden and abstruse things. Probably, you can decipher what it says. All the men are well, and are feeling jolly. We may be ready to return in a week. I hope the old ship is coming along all right.

"Hurriedly, as ever,
"BLAKELY."

"That is satisfactory. Blakely is the right man for his job," remarked John.

"Now, let us see what the scrap has to say," said the Professor.

John held the scrap up to the light, and all peered at it. "I think there are cross lines on it, although I am not quite sure," he said, as he again held it up so the light could flash through it.

"What difference would that make whether it had or it hadn't cross lines?" asked Harry.

"Simply this: I wanted to satisfy myself whether or not it was taken from a ship's pad, which is generally ruled both ways."

"What is the object of having paper ruled both ways?"

"It is a convenient way of making calculations where measurements are necessary, as is the case in figuring out and placing the different celestial marks which guide the sailors. I think this is a marine pad. Now, let us see what it contains, before we go further."

"See the name signed at the bottom," cried out George. "W-a-l-t. That must be a 't'. But the rest is blurred."

"I wonder if that isn't Walter?" said Harry.

"Who is Walter?" asked John.

"Walter? Why he is the man who signed the note we found on the *Investigator's* life boat No. 3 and from whom we have never heard."

"I remember now," said John, reflectively. "He mentioned Wright who was one of my companions. But I did not know Walter,—but what is this?" All craned forward now. "Here is a line; it looks like a large V, pointing to the south;—that is if the upper part of the paper is the north."

"There is some sort of tracing on it," said George.

"Your eyesight is good, George, see if you can see any figures on the sheet that will explain the V, and the reason for the name below."

"There is the slightest sign of a figure, or a word just below the point of the V. It looks like '30'. This seems to be an arrow, which points to the right diagonally."

"Now you boys have something to occupy your minds. Yon have been interested in the Walter note for a year; now is the time to do some investigating."

"I have an idea," said Harry, jumping up. "Where can we find the original Walter's note? We can compare the signature, and that will tell whether it is Walter or not."

The Professor smiled as he noticed the eagerness of the boys. They rushed out of the room and went over to the shop to reclaim the note that had given them so much concern fourteen months before.

When they had gone John said: "I presume you have already guessed what the note contains?"

"Unquestionably it has reference to the location of the main ledge of copper or other ore which is measured from some point in that vicinity, and which may be determined later on by noting the place where the missive was found, or from some natural landmark."

"That is my view, but I felt it would be better for the boys to dig it out for themselves," replied John.

The wonderful nature of the instruction which the boys had

obtained during their stay on the island, was characterized by this little incident. Everything learned by one's own exertions is not only more valuable because of that fact, but the facts thus gleaned will leave a stronger impress upon the mind.

The boys thus learned by doing things themselves, that they became strong and self reliant, and it made them happy to think that they were able to pick up the threads, however tangled, and weave them into a harmonious whole. It is the secret of doing things well.

CHAPTER III

THE ARROW ON THE SHEET

When the boys reached their rooms they set to work to decipher the colored paper. It was about four by six inches in size, and had been folded twice, as the creases plainly showed. Assuring themselves that it was paper which had been crossruled, as suggested by John, they tried to decipher the straggling letters and form them into some coherent form.

The paper had the following appearance when they received it:

The words, or parts of words "dire," in the first line, and "30 gues" in the second line, together with the letters "Walt" are the only absolutely clear things to be noticed.

"The writing is right across the V-shaped marks, and the arrow is plain enough. It may be though, that the arrow has nothing to do with the V-shaped mark." And George held the paper away from his eyes to get the proper effect at a distance.

"I wonder how close the mountain is to the sea?" ventured Harry.

"I don't see what difference that would make," replied George. "That *30* must mean some measurement. It is either feet, or miles, or yards, or,—"

"Why can't you see that 'gues' is a part of the word 'leagues.'"

Harry jumped up as though shot. "Well, that was stupid of us, sure enough."

"With that key before us, we can make some headway. I believe the V-shape is the lower end of the mountain, probably a headland, and the arrow points to a place 30 leagues to the,—see here, in the last line is a W. and there is a blur before it and after it. That may be SWE, EWS, SWW, SWS, and,—"

"Don't go so fast," shrieked Harry. "What do you suppose the capital I stands for at the beginning of the third line?"

"I—I—, why,—*Island*, of course," said George, with an air of superiority. "But it cannot be west."

"Well, the arrow points southeast."

"How do you know?" asked George, dubiously.

"Why, that word at the extreme top must be 'north,' and if so then the arrow is pointing south, and the 'W' belongs to something in that direction."

"There, in the second line is a word that looks like 'land.' Can it be a part of the word 'Island'?"

"It doesn't seem so, as there is too much space before the letters. It seems to me though, that it reads 'land 30 leagues' but what does 'se' mean?"

The boys were up late that night, and they went to bed with the missive still unsolved. Before retiring Harry said: "Let us wait until daylight. The sun may help us out."

When they awoke the first thing that occurred to George was the original Walter letter, so that the writing could be compared. It was found, and George came in with an exultant bound.

"I am sure now that it was Walter. Here it is." The original letter was as follows:

Go directly south from the large river which flows to the east, west of the mountains. We are too closely watched to escape. The tribe at war with our captors are to the west of. If I escape I will follow the river to the sea so you will understand where I am.

Walter.

"Compare the two and you will see they look alike," said George.

"What shall we tell the Professor!" asked Harry.

"Well but I am not yet through with the paper. Suppose we moisten it, and that may bring out something we didn't see before."

This was done, but it made the entire document worse than before.

"Too bad we have spoiled it," remarked Harry, "but I think we are safe in telling the Professor and John what we have found out."

For the time being, however, the boys had other urgent work to do. The day for launching had been set, and every working hour was valuable, so they were over at the ship yard early, and the boys did not see either John or the Professor during the day.

The vessel as designed by Harry, and supervised by John, was ninety feet long, and had a beam of eighteen feet, with a very deep keel, and high bulwarks. It was constructed of a species of oak, found in abundance in the forest west of the town, and was cut up into boards, and dried in specially-prepared kilns which were put up for the purpose.

While lumber dried in this way is not the best for ordinary uses, it will serve for shipping purposes, because there is always more or less moisture present in the hull of the vessel, and the object was to enable them to get the material in the speediest way.

The saw mill was one of their first experiments in building machinery, and it was in constant service from the day it was first erected, getting out lumber for building purposes.

The engine was designed only for auxiliary purposes, and the boiler was intended to use coal, of which they found an ample supply in the northern portion of the island, as explained in a previous book.

When the boys returned to their rooms late that afternoon, the first thing that interested them was the message. When it was brought in it was dry, and a slight change was noticed in its appearance. Now, what appeared to be the first word of the message, was discernible, the word "Take," and the word "Head" could be made out before and as a part of "land," in the second line.

"We have it," cried Harry, as he jumped up. "Now let them know about it."

They were across the open space, without any ceremony, and without taking trouble to announce themselves, were in the Professor's room.

"We have it,—we have made it out," was the announcement, as Harry held up the message.

"Does it tell you where the Copper mine is located?" asked the Professor.

"Copper mine!" exclaimed George. "What has a copper mine to do with it?"

"John and I concluded, from certain markings on the paper, that it contained a diagram of the mine!"

"Well, you were mistaken," said Harry with a chuckle. "It is something about an island, thirty leagues to the southeast, somewhere."

"Is that so?" exclaimed the Professor in surprise. "Get John. He will be surprised."

John came hurriedly at the announcement, and the contents of the missive pointed out. "This is certainly good news," he said. "That was fine work on your part."

"You see the arrow, and the part of the word 'leagues.' That couldn't mean feet or yards, or miles."

"Quite evident," said John, as he mused for a while. "This confirms, in a measure, the information that we have as to the proximity of these islands, but the charts show them farther away."

"Undoubtedly, if Walter knew what he was talking about, we have an interesting problem to decipher, and the determination to make the voyage is a wise and timely one," interposed the Professor.

"Now for the ship," said Harry. "Every day is a hundred, in my mind."

As may be imagined, the boys now worked with feverish haste. Other islands here, and waiting for them! Sometimes they were almost tempted to give up the trip home, but the Professor would not hear of it.

"Do not change your plans, if you have any good conclusions when you start out. Don't oscillate from one thing to another. Always make up your minds and then take a wise, persistent course. It is that which always serves you best."

"No; we will go home first, and *then* for the islands," said Harry, who felt relieved that the impetuous nature of George could be brought to their way of thinking, although George was by far the most homesick of the entire lot.

All the boys were on hand when the vessel was launched. It rode the water beautifully, and the natives were the most enthusiastic helpers. They felt proud of their work. Uraso and Muro, the two chiefs, who were the most prominent men in the community, and particularly Sutoto, the intelligent Beree, and Stut, the brother-in-law of Muro, were on hand.

It was a great feast day for the people. Tears actually flowed from the Professor's eyes, as he saw the women and children crowd about him. He was almost a God to them. They were accustomed to receive visits from him in his weekly rounds, and how at such times he loved to tell them how to make and arrange things about the house, which contributed to their comfort.

Everybody was at work; all were happy, and no one appreciated this more than the women, who had been lifted out of the bonds of slavery and elevated through the wise administration of the Professor.

Angel, too, was in evidence. He was the first to climb the mast, as the ship floated in the stream.

"I wonder whether Angel remembers the first trip he took with us on boat No. 1?" asked Harry.

Angel bestowed a knowing look on Harry. "I believe he knows what you said," remarked George.

In another week the rigging had been put up, and the boiler and engine were installed before the launching, so that the necessary work required to enable the ship to sail, was the provisioning. John suggested that what was of far more importance would be the work of training a crew to handle the ship, so they turned their minds toward the solution of this question.

The selection of a crew was a most difficult task, because all the men were willing to volunteer. It was decided, however, that only the unmarried men should be taken, and this at once eliminated many who might otherwise have been selected.

For three days the ship was taken out to sea, under sail only,and John found no trouble in maneuvering the vessel with his new crew. John was a sailor, and had once been owner of a vessel, so that they were in competent hands.

But the final day came, when they must go. It was a most trying time for the poor boys. Almost at the last moment, Harry and George walked back to the Professor's room, and broke out into tears.

"Everybody is leaving you," said Harry, "and I cannot bear to go and leave you in this way."

All the rescued boys were on board, as well as Blakely, since the Professor had insisted that the latter should go, for business reasons, so that the Professor was left alone, the only white man on Wonder Island, when the ship sailed down the river.

True, there was no reason to fear for his safety. The natives loved him too devotedly, but the boys felt that he must often be lonely in his new surroundings, with no one but the natives about him. They little knew that the solace and comfort of the grand old man was the knowledge that he had helped his fellow man, though the color of the skin was darker than his own.

* * * * *

Their voyage was accompanied by favoring winds and perfect weather. Valparaiso, Chile, was the first port at which they landed, and as a trip around the Horn, or even through the Straits of Magellan, and up along the Atlantic coast, would mean several months, with their own vessel, they shipped in one of the line steamers, and within seven weeks they saw Sandy Hook lightship, and then the forts which lined the opposite shore at the Narrows.

Telegrams to their parents created paroxysms of joy in many

homes which had been robbed when the *Investigator* went down. There were no happier homes than the ones Harry and George were welcomed to.

The papers told the stories of the boys in pages and pages of descriptions, and they showed the photos, and told what the boys had done in their temporary home. The hero of all this wonderful home-coming was Angel.

The people, the houses, the wonderful automobiles which he saw on every hand, at first alarmed him, but when he saw that George did not seem a bit afraid, he reconciled himself to the situation.

His first automobile ride was a revelation to him. He held on tightly to George, at first, but soon the sensation became one of joy, and he could not get enough of it. The boys were certainly feted, but when they told their parents that they must go back, the proposition met with strong opposition.

The parents forgot that the boys were now over two years older than when they went away, and it seemed singular that the surroundings did not seem the same to them as before the happy boyhood days before they left home.

For business reasons the parents knew that it would be prudent to permit them to return and they were influenced by the remarkable change they saw in the manners and actions of the boys. They saw the youths were strong and self reliant, ever ready to act and to carry out their resolutions. These boys had been transformed into men.

They spent many days going over old scenes and visiting friends. They enjoyed to the utmost the reunion with their families, but they could not cease talking about the Professor. They now realized in full what he had been to them, and what his example and teaching meant to them. There was really a feeling amounting almost to jealousy on the part of the people at home against the Professor, but it was not one of bitterness.

One who could exert such a healthy influence on the lives of the young, as he possessed, was worthy of the adulation that the boys bestowed. But John was not forgotten in these periods of happiness.

They were never happy when telling the tales of their adventures except when John was present, and the latter was the most sought-for individual, because when he once began to tell some of his vivid tales the people would not let him stop.

Finally the time for departure came. A merry party gathered upon the dock when the explorers were about to depart. They would write at least once a month, as Blakely had assured them that he would arrange to have a steamer run a round trip each four weeks, to take care of the commodities which would be made up by the natives.

The steamship *Panama* slowly moved out into the bay, and the boys remembered the memorable event which took place at that same dock thirty months before. Then they left with a sort of half joy in their hearts, and now they were going away to finish up the great adventures which they had started when they reached the island of Wonder.

All hearts were anxious as the ship neared Valparaiso, because there they would leave the liner from New York, and again ship in the boat they had built. They keenly scanned the pier as the vessel was being warped in.

"Ah! there is Blakely on the dock," said Harry.

"But I don't see the *Pioneer* here!" responded George.

Pioneer was the name of the vessel they had built, and which brought them to that port from their island home.

The moment the vessel came alongside the dock, George called to Blakely: "Where is our boat?"

"At Wonder Island," was the reply.

"At Wonder Island?" said Harry, and the boys looked at each other in amazement. And now they must wait several weeks, probably, until it returns. This was disappointing, indeed.

The boys rushed off. "And where shall we go now?" asked Harry.

"Over to our ship," replied Blakely.

They followed his gaze to a dock beyond, where lay a beautiful vessel, a steamer, all decked out with flags.

"Is that our vessel!"

"Yes, and I have been to Wonder Island on her since you left. We just arrived two days ago. We are ready to steam out within two hours."

"Then don't let us waste a moment's time," said Harry.

"I thought you might want to take a look over the town," said Blakely.

"I have no wish to do so, as long as we have the islands in view," remarked George. "And how is the Professor," he continued in an eager tone.

"He is well and happy. But I have no doubt he longs for you, as he frequently goes over to your rooms, and wanders around the shop, a thing which he never did while you were there."

This was joyful news to the boys. How they longed to sail up Enterprise River. The steamer which Blakely had bought, and which was destined to ply between Wonder Island and the nearest trans-shipping point, was called the *Wonder*, a thing which the boys had not noticed until they were nearing the vessel.

It was a saucy little steamer, and as they drew near Blakely said: "What speed do you think she will make?"

"Fifteen miles at least," remarked Harry.

"I am guaranteed eighteen miles an hour at the least."

"Isn't that fine," said George. "What does she burn?"

"Either wood, coal or petroleum."

"Now would be the time to look up the oil deposits on the island," remarked Harry.

Within an hour the ship was under way, greatly to the delight of the boys.

Notwithstanding the ship was sent forward under full steam, the speed was far too slow for the impatient boys. They were on the bridge most of the time with the Captain who had been employed to run the vessel. He proved to be a jolly, red-faced tar, who loved the antics of the boys.

CHAPTER IV

THE SKULL WITH THE CRYPTIC WRITING

It was at the latter part of May when the *Wonder* steamed up the broad river which led to the town of Unity. When they were within two miles of the town, where they could begin to see the beautiful white houses in the distance, Blakely came up to the bridge, and suggested that it would be time to give the town a salute.

The Captain gave the order and the great whistle began to make a horrible din, and kept it up for a full half mile. Long before the boat came into sight of the dock itself the boys could see the people of the town hurrying down to the wharf.

When they saw the boys on the bridge pandemonium was let loose.

"This looks and acts just like a real American town," said Harry.

"See the Professor," said Harry, as he rushed to the end of the bridge, and frantically waved his hat.

The plank was swung and fastened, and the crew of natives rushed off and met their friends, but George and Harry were not permitted to walk down the gang plank. The joy at seeing them again was so intense that the people took them on their shoulders, and the Professor had a hard time to get near enough to grasp them and bid a welcome.

The people marveled at the boys. They were dressed up in regulation American style, and the Professor asked them if they had brought the "latest" cuts to put in the show windows.

Everybody followed, and the bantering and cheering made a continuous performance for them until they reached their home. All the chiefs were there, dressed up for the occasion, and what delighted them more than anything else was the fact that the Krishnos, the former witch doctors of the tribes, and who were now the teachers for the children, were the first to offer congratulations on their return.

There was no work in the town that day. Everybody determined to celebrate, and it was with hearts full of joy that the boys witnessed the demonstrations in their behalf.

"Isn't this a glorious home-coming?" said George. "It was worth the trip here to witness it."

"It does seem strange to call it a 'home-coming,' but that is just what it is," answered Harry. "How happy the people are. They seem to appreciate everything that has been done for them, and it is such a pleasure to do things for those who appreciate it."

The stories which John brought to the Professor were so beguiling that he promised the boys that he would probably be able during the next year to make a visit with them to their homes, and this delighted them beyond measure.

Although they had been absent four months, they noted many improvements made during their absence. The boys, on their own initiative, visited many of the homes, and talked to the people, and told them of the visit home. And how those simple people enjoyed this kindly act, and cherished it for months afterwards.

But it was now time to think seriously of the contemplated voyage of discovery, which was ever uppermost in the minds of the boys. While conversing on the subject a few evenings after their return, Harry remarked: "I suppose we must use the *Pioneer* for our trip, as the *Wonder* will have to make the regular trips?"

"John and I think that would be the wisest plan. The native sailors are now well adapted to handle her, and do you know that Sutoto sailed her around the island?"

This was pleasing to the boys, who liked Sutoto.

"And who are the others that went with him?"

"Why Lolo was one of them, and Stut and Chump. Oh, they had a jolly time; so they said, and I can believe it, because they are simply crazy to make another trip." And the Professor beamed as he related many of the incidents which they told him of their experiences.

While they were talking, Sutoto appeared, and was immediately admitted. After some talk, Sutoto said: "The Professor said that when you returned you would have some work for me with the *Pioneer*."

"Yes, and you shall command her," said Harry.

Sutoto could not but show his pleasure. "I knew you would

come back, but so many here said you would not."

At this point Professor explained that there were many rumors among the people to the effect that the boys would never again come back, and all showed grief at the news. I assured them that you were just as anxious to return as they were to have you and I then told Sutoto that I knew you had plans which would require his services, but I thought it would be more agreeable if you imparted the nature of it to him.

The boys were not slow to outline the plans to him, but advised him to keep the information to himself, which he promised to do. It was enough for him to know that he would command the ship. It was this that induced Sutoto to take out the ship, and finally to circumnavigate the island, so as to try out the sailors and properly to fit them for the work when the boys returned.

"Now that being settled, Sutoto, we are going to leave the work of provisioning the *Pioneer* to you. We must take a supply of guns and ammunition, as well, and probably it would be wise to have a small troop of the best soldiers," was Harry's instruction.

"Uraso wants to go. I am sure he would be the best one to take.

"What will Muro say to that?" asked the Professor.

"Oh, take him along, by all means," said George, "because I want Lolo to go with us."

It was then settled that they were to take a small force, sufficient for immediate purposes, and if it was found that the islands discovered were too well settled with hostiles it would be an easy matter to remain aloof, or return for reinforcements.

While arrangements were being made for the departure of the expedition Blakely informed the Professor that it would be good policy to make up part of the cargo of the *Wonder* with copper, and that both vessels could proceed to the southeastern part of the island, and the men aboard could be used to transport the copper to the sea.

In this way the expedition would serve a double purpose. No one attempted to go contrary to the wishes of Blakely on matters which touched upon the commercial ventures in which they were engaged.

John was only too glad that Blakely had hit upon that idea, as he was anxious to visit that part of the coast, contiguous to the copper deposit, and what was more, he wanted to see the place where Blakely found the missive which the boys had translated.

As there was still a week before the *Wonder* would sail for its northern port of call, both of the ships wended their way to the east, skirting the coast as closely as possible, John on the *Pioneer* with the boys.

They now had an opportunity to see the Great South Mountains from the sea. They remembered when they last saw them on land, during the campaign against the Illyas, and also the wonderful village on the western side of the mountains. What would their present wanderings bring forth?

That evening they landed within a cove, both vessels being brought as near the shore as possible.

"We can safely go in close this evening, because the tide is now out," said John.

Sutoto, while he had navigated the vessel, and had shown remarkable skill, was, nevertheless, not well versed in tides and the action of the moon.

Quick to learn, he asked John why the tides thus changed. John explained the reason that the tides flowed in and out twice during each twenty-four hours, or a little less than that time, so that high water, or low water would always be at a time a little later each day, and then stated that it would be an easy matter to so make the calculations that they would be able to tell ahead for a whole year just when during each day the highest or lowest water would be.

While waiting on the ship during the hours of the evening they were interested in the magnificent fire flies which they saw on the shore and along the mountain side. This was not an unfamiliar sight to them as they had witnessed such scenes many times before.

But now they saw such sights as they had never before observed. They must have been giant glow birds, because some of the lights flew at least hundreds of feet emitting continuous streams of light, and this was not all, many of the lights were colored, particularly red and blue or simply faint tinges of those tints.

"I have often thought that there is nothing more wonderful than the fire fly," said George.

"But what do you think makes it so wonderful?" asked John.

"Well, I suppose the wonderful part is that it has strength enough to make a light," answered Harry.

"No, the remarkable thing is that the light which it emits is absolutely cool. Experiments which have been made go to show that there is no heat. In every form of light which man has been able to produce thus far artificially, a great heat is evolved, and it would be a most valuable discovery to find out why these insects are able to do it without raising the temperature."

"But what difference does it make if heat is produced?" asked Harry.

"The production of heat means the loss of power. The heat generated takes up more of the power than the light which is produced, so that it would be a great economy if the heat could be dispensed with."

"But if there was no heat in the light produced would it make any difference in the lamps themselves?"

"Unquestionably. The lamps would last much longer."

"What are the things which must be learned in order to get the secret of cold light?"

"Well, there are number of questions which must be determined. While it is known that the fire fly and the glow worm emit what is called a phosphorescent light, this fact is a mere prelude to the knowledge of what is the exact color of daylight."

"Color of Daylight? Why, I supposed it was white."

"But the light of the glow worm and fire fly are not white."

They watched them, and soon appreciated that John's statement was true.

"You asked what were some of the things to be solved? Well, to find out the secret of the phosphorescent glow. That is one thing. What is the best artificial light, is the next. Then, what substance will have the most intense glow when a current passes through it, and give out the least heat."

"Well, has no one attempted to explain any of these things?"

"Yes; many explanations have been offered, but all of them leave the subject dark somewhere." And John laughed as he saw that the boys appreciated his little attempt at witticism.

"But the time will come when man will find out this, as everything in his way. When you think of it, that electricians, chemists, metallurgists, physiologists, engineers, physicists and microscopists, are all working on the problem, we should be able to extract the secret sooner or later."

"I am going to have some of those fellows," shouted George, and when the natives on board heard the request of George there was a scramble for the boats, and John was delighted to give them instructions for capturing the insects.

Early the next day the entire party landed, and Blakely, together with John and the boys, started for the high peak, the one visible for miles from the west, and which John and the boys often wished to visit.

One of the things which the boys brought with them from the States, was a pair of strong glasses, and these were constantly in use.

"What do you say to scaling that point?" said Harry.

"Just what I have been thinking about," said George.

Sutoto, who was with the party, showed by his glowing eyes that he wanted to be of the party. "Certainly you shall go," said Harry.

"Before going we must visit the place where the Walter note was found," called out John.

The boys had forgotten this. "Most assuredly," answered George, "I had almost forgotten that."

Blakely led the way up alongside the rugged cliff. "See that bluish green outcropping," he said as they were pulling themselves up.

John stopped and chipped off some specimens. "Wonderful!" he exclaimed. "Better than anything I have ever found in Mexico. These hills remind me of the formation all along western Chihuahua, and through northeastern Sonora."

The ledge on which they finally emerged was fully six hundred feet above sea level. When they turned around and viewed the sea below them, and saw the ships at anchor, they were delirious with joy. How Sutoto enjoyed the scene. He had never seen anything like it before and he was amazed and stupefied. He turned and grasped George by the hand. He was too full to speak.

"But wait, Sutoto, until we get to the top," said Harry, as he saw his countenance. As they looked up at the top they wondered what they might see from the elevation.

"Here is the spot," cried out Blakely. "This is the pot in which the message was found. And here is something that I dug up afterwards."

The boys crowded around. It was a skull on which was

engraved the characters ABCC, followed by a star.

All looked at John, thinking he might offer some solution. He turned it over, and examined every portion. Not a word was spoken. "Tell me the exact position in which this was found," he asked, as he looked at Blakely.

"The first thing I found was the pot, which was simply turned upside down, in exactly this way. This is the place. It rested on this flat stone. The skull was behind it on this upper shelf."

"And was there nothing else on the shelf?"

"Nothing whatever."

John stooped down and carefully examined the shelf. All followed his motions. "Do you see that mark?" he said, pointing to a heavy scratch, which was now plain. "That mark is associated with the skull, if not with the message. I am unable at this time fully to decipher the marks on the skull, but I have an idea of the meaning."

"I wonder if the scratch across that is in the same direction as the arrow in the letter?" asked George.

"Unquestionably: let me see your glasses," and George unslung them as John took them and gazed long in the direction of the line on the shelf.

He lowered the glasses and slowly shook his head. Something was forming itself in his mind, this was evident. He walked around the ledge and back again. Finally, he said: "I wish it were night, it might help to solve the riddle."

"And why?" asked Harry.

"Those letters have reference to the star which follows."

"It seems to me to be a singular thing that anyone should leave this here in the hope or expectation that it could be a guide for any one," remarked George.

"There is certainly one explanation of that," answered John. "It is evident that the articles were placed there as a form of note to others, and it is a sort of cryptic sign, intelligible only to those who have the key. The fact that these signs are here denote several things, one of which is that something important, such, for instance, as treasures, or the location of hidden wealth, or the directions necessary to find mining lodes, or even to point out the direction and distances of other islands in the distance."

"But," said Harry, "the fact that we have found these things here looks as though there were other parties besides Walter and that he was associated with them in some sort of enterprise."

"Quite true; but I am not at all satisfied that the Walter note has anything to do with the skull. In fact there is every evidence to me that they are entirely disconnected with each other."

This announcement was the most surprising to Blakely, who now added a few points of information. "I should have said that the skull was not exposed as you now see it on the shelf. After I went up the side of the hill, I returned and landed on the ledge, and then I noticed the skull through the apertures formed by the stones now lying at the side."

"That is evidence to my mind, that Walter knew nothing of the existence of the skull at the time he left the message, and yet, singular as it may seem, both the skull and Walter's message point to the same thing."

This announcement was certainly curious and interesting, and keyed up the listeners to a high pitch of expectation.

CHAPTER V

THE TRIP TO THE NEW ISLAND

Exciting as were the events alluded to in the last chapter, the boys insisted on taking Sutoto to the top of the peak. John and Blakely gathered up the fragments, and when the boys left they were busily engaged in making careful measurements of the stone and ledges.

It was not an easy task to gain the summit, but when they reached it, there was spread before them the most remarkable panorama. To the north they could see South River, the first stream they discovered when they came to the island.

They looked on it almost lovingly. "If it were not for the mountain range to the north we could see clear to Cataract," said Harry.

"The dear old place!" exclaimed George. Sutoto smiled. He had been there, and he shared the views of the boys.

"Let me have the glasses," shouted Harry, as he adjusted them and turned to the west. "Unity," was the only thing he said, as he handed the glasses to Sutoto. The latter looked, and stepped back in surprise. George kept his eyes on Sutoto, as the latter bent forward in his eagerness to see the town which was now so plain to him, although more than fifty miles away.

George leisurely took the glasses, as Sutoto said slowly, and with proper emphasis, "Wonderful! wonderful!"

He turned the glasses to the southeast, hoping to catch a glimpse of the land of treasures, but they saw nothing but the wide open sea, calm and peaceful, and he wondered that it could ever be so angry and tempestuous as they had known it to be on two momentous occasions.

They remained there for a long time, and viewed every portion of the island. When they descended they took a route leading to the west, and when nearly at the bottom, heard the unmistakable sounds of voices below them. For a moment the boys were alarmed, but Sutoto set up a shout, his quick ears having detected the voices of their friends. It was the first caravan load of copper which they were taking from the great cave near the Illyas' village.

"Glory! we are near the Illyas' village," said Harry, as he stumbled down the mountain side, and saw the train of men with the loads.

They would now do some more visiting. They must surely go over to the village where they captured the last of the hostile tribes. As they neared the village they were surprised to see Oma coming toward them. He greeted them like a monarch, and led them into the village.

"I am glad to welcome you," he said. The boys were astounded at the words. This man, the most vindictive and bitter of all the tribesmen, had learned to speak, and showed by his actions that he was glad to welcome them.

But when they came to the village, the surprise of the boys was so great that they could hardly speak. Instead of filth and uncleanliness everywhere, they saw carefully attended lawns, and houses, instead of huts. The people came out and greeted them with laughter.

And then the boys recognized many of the men who had lived in Unity, and who had worked for them in the shops, and in the fields. The Chief then escorted them to the large building, the same one in which the Chief was captured by the boys, the year before.

What a change! Formerly the furniture in the room was one jumbled mass of debris, and the household arrangements were only such as savage conditions warranted. Now, the large interior had been cut up into rooms, and they were furnished with comfortable belongings.

The Chief saw the curiosity of the boys, and he read their thoughts. "You wonder at the difference? Yes; it is a difference. We owe it to that wonderful Chief, and to you, and to John."

"Yes; John will be here soon," said George.

"I have seen him. He will be here. We are preparing a great feast for him," and the boys opened their eyes and smiled as they heard this announcement.

The people flocked about them, and the men who knew the boys were only too proud to be recognized by them. Thus they visited every nook and corner of the town, surprised and glad to see that the Chief had insisted on his people going to Unity and learning the ways of the white people.

There was a further reason why the coming of John and of

Blake was a joyous event. Oma had been informed that the great copper mines were to be opened in the mountains, which would insure work for every one, and that they would be able to buy every sort of luxury and enjoy all the comforts of the white people.

Late that evening John and Blakely came accompanied by two hundred of the Illyas who had actually been engaged during the day in transporting copper from the cave to the hold of the *Wonder*.

The feast and the celebration that night in a village which, only a few months before, was of the most savage character, was, indeed, a marvel. Oma could scarcely express himself with enough earnestness, and the women were following the boys with their eyes, and actually caressing them, in their eagerness to show appreciation.

When the time came for them to leave, the Chief accompanied the men to the shore below South Mountain to witness their departure. Before they left the village, the things which had been brought there by the ships for the Illyas were placed in the Chief's storehouse, and Blakely paid the members of the party who had assisted them. This, also, was the occasion for much rejoicing.

Blakely, on board the *Wonder*, waved an adieu to the boys and John as the boats separated, and Sutoto gave the order to sail directly southeast.

During the afternoon the sea was calm and afforded a beautiful sail, but during the night a strong breeze came up and its intensity varied during the night. The next day, however, the sea became choppy, and over two-thirds of the natives were rolling around on the deck in the agonies of seasickness.

"This will give us an opportunity to try the new cure for the malady," said John.

"What is that?" asked George.

"Simply atrophine."

"How is it administered?"

"By injecting it."

"What is atrophine?" asked Harry.

"It is a crystalline, bitter and poisonous alkaloid, taken from the deadly nightshade, and the same principle is also found in the thorn apple."

"Isn't it the same as belladonna?" remarked George.

"No; but belladonna is also an extract of nightshade."

"Have you any of it here?"

"Yes; I brought some, together with the other drugs that the Professor ordered, and I am anxious to try it. The remedy was discovered by Prof. Fischer, of Munich, and also simultaneously by Dr. Reginald Pollard, of South Kensington, England."

Accompanied by the boys John went among the sufferers, and administered the medicine, giving at each injection about 1-64th of a grain. It was remarkable in its effects. Within a half hour the sickening feeling in the stomach disappeared, the eyes began to grow bright again, the pulse full, and the patient became strong and vigorous.

None of them objected to John's ministrations. Their confidence in his ability was sufficient for them and the results justified their faith.

When the boys came on deck in the morning, they strained their eyes looking toward the horizon for land but there was no land in sight. John was already on deck and he smiled as he saw them ascend the ladder. "And where is your island?" he asked.

"How far have we gone?"

"We have been driven somewhat out of our course, it is true; but we are more than a hundred miles from Wonder Island, and have sailed past the place where the other island ought to be, according to Walter's letter." And John chuckled somewhat, at the crestfallen looks of the boys.

"Where are we going now?"

"I told Sutoto we would better tack to the southwest. We can use up a day at that course, and then double back, probably thirty or forty miles to the south, and in that way we can cover a wide area."

While sailing in that direction they had to go pretty much into the face of the wind, but it was considered wise to explore that region to the south of the islands first, and then take another section to the east or to the west.

Night came on without any indications of land, and the course was altered directly to the east. The boys remained up until nearly twelve that night, but no light or evidence of land came in sight. Tired with the exertions of the day, they retired, and were soon asleep.

How long they slept was immaterial to them. Sutoto came into their cabin, and awakened them, saying, "We can see some lights in the east." They heard the voice, and its earnest expression, and without waiting to dress scrambled out. Far off to the southeast was a faint glimmer, then it died away.

After a moment or two it appeared again, somewhat brighter than before. The night was intensely dark, and the wind was blowing a steady gale, so that the boat not only rocked but it moved forward into the lines of waves across their path.

John was above, and they hurriedly rushed to see him. He was smiling, as they approached, and he greeted them by saying "We have reached your island, probably."

"How long have you seen the light?" asked George.

"A half hour, or more," he answered.

The boys were not in the mood now to return to bed, so they went back to dress, and then returned, meanwhile watching the light with eager eyes. The course of the ship was directed toward it, and every one on board had now heard the news.

Soon the watch on the port side sang out: "Land ahead," and every one sprang to the left side. There, plainly in the darkness, was a headland, or a spur, which they were passing at almost right angles. The most intense excitement prevailed.

Still the light was directly ahead, and, apparently, a long distance from them. John told Sutoto to haul in the sails, and to take a course directly to the south. He explained that it would be wise to stand off the shore as long as possible, as the ship's clock showed that it was now past four o'clock so that within the next hour they might be able to view the land clearly enough to determine their future course.

Impatiently they awaited that period of gloom which is said to be the darkest time,—just before the dawn. This seemed to be so to the watchers, but shortly after five the curtain lifted. A slight haze was over the land, but they had found an island, at least.

"Do you know our position?" asked Harry, as John approached. "Yes; I have just figured it out. We are fifty leagues (one hundred and fifty miles) southeast of Wonder Island."

The boys looked at each other. Evidently Walter was wrong, or they had read his letter incorrectly. But they saw land, and John assured them that there was no land between that place and their own island.

Anxiously they awaited daylight, and when it came they gazed out on a barren waste,—a rocky and uninviting shore.

"Steer for the little cove beyond the great rock," said John.

The sails were hoisted, and the vessel slowly moved south, and rounded into the waters bounded by the circular shore line. The anchor was soon cast, and then began the launching of the boats.

John called the men before him, and gave a few words of advice. "We have no knowledge of the character of the land, or of the people who may live there. Two boats will be manned, and ten will take their places in each. Uraso will have charge of one, and Muro of the other. When we reach the shore Muro will remain with the men under his command, while Uraso will follow me. It will be understood that so long as no shots are heard by Muro and his party that our expedition is safe, but should any firing be heard, then the ship must be signaled and those in the vessel here must come to shore, and Muro with his soldiers will at once come to our relief. I hope we shall have no occasion for calling on you, but we must be prepared for any emergency."

The two boats pulled for the shore. After landing John, with Uraso's men the boys quickly scrambled up the rough cliffs beyond. When the heights were gained they looked over a beautifully wooded landscape, but it was still, except for the birds and the small animals which looked at them in a startled manner, and then scurried for cover.

"I doubt whether there are any people living here," remarked Harry. "There is not a sign of living beings."

"You are quite mistaken there," said John.

The boys looked at John. "Have you seen any signs?" asked George.

"Yes; did you notice how the animals fled at our approach?"

They had noticed it, but neglected to draw any inference from it.

"That is one of the surest signs. Do you now remember how differently the animals acted in the region around Cataract from those in the southwest portion of Wonder Island?"

"I now remember that is so. Don't you remember, George, when we came across the first herd of yaks, that they hardly noticed us? I am sure that the animals out at West River didn't wait to interview us."

"Well, I remember the big bear was very anxious to make our acquaintance," said George, and Harry smiled, as he remembered how the big fellow took his revenge by tearing up their baggage.

John directed the men to the right, and in the direction of an elevation which seemed to be clear of timber. From that point they searched the intervening wooded area, and caught sight of a still higher tableland miles beyond.

"Your glasses would be serviceable here," said John. George handed them to John, and he gazed through them long and earnestly. "I am unable to find any traces of human beings, and I cannot account for the light which we saw during the night, and which must have been nearly ahead of us."

He walked forward, the men following. They marched for more than a mile, every object being examined. Fallen trees were particularly investigated, and clumps of trees were searched, even the bark of trees being minutely gone over by John.

The natives, generally so keen to discover evidences of their kind, walked along, and shook their heads, to indicate the absence of all signs. The land in the interior was elevated, but it was not rough or broken, the only place where an upheaval had taken place appearing to be the west coast.

"This seems to look bad for our purposes," said John, as he turned to the boys.

"What do you mean?" asked Harry.

"I don't think there are any caves in this section," he answered. "But we might as well investigate farther to the right, and see what the land looks like."

"Aren't those coffee trees?" said George, in great eagerness, as he bounded forwardly.

There, not a hundred feet away, were the beautiful trees with white clusters all over them. Thousands of these trees were in sight.

"I believe we have struck a coffee plantation," exclaimed Harry.

John did not answer, but went up to one of the trees and carefully examined it. "No, these trees have grown wild, and no one has ever gathered the berries."

"But what an opportunity there would be here for gathering coffee! Too bad Blakely isn't here," said George.

"We never saw anything like it on Wonder Island," suggested Harry. "Now, why is it that cocoa will grow in wonderful profusion on one island, and none on the next, and the other island will have bananas and the other not?"

"The explanation of that has been the means of bringing out a wonderful study, that is explained by the nature of the soil itself. In every country certain sections will spontaneously produce product alike, in almost every essential quality. Thus, flax, for instance, is found, identical in its character, in Kamscatska, and in Minnesota; in the Siberian wilds and in Central America; on the heights of the Himalayas, and in the lowest plains of South America."

"But how do you explain the similarity? They must have come from seed, and how did the seeds get from place to place, when there were no ships to carry them?"

"There can be only one explanation. The soil itself, if identical in its character, will, eventually, produce the same vegetables and vegetation. Thus, it has been found that the localities where this wild flax was found, had soil which was the same in its nature, and calculated to produce the same in kind."

For four hours the little band marched to the south, and came back along a track nearer the sea, without discovering the slightest indication of human habitations, except the frightened looks and actions of the animals in their path.

CHAPTER VI

DISCOVERY OF THE ISLAND
AND EXPLORATIONS

Weary, they dragged themselves over the cliffs and down to the waiting natives. Muro was surprised to learn that they had found no signs of people, so they rowed back to the ship, and after a hearty meal, retired for the night.

In the morning when they asked John for his opinion, he said, "The only course is to sail south, and circumnavigate the island. In doing so we shall effect a landing every ten miles or so, and then go into the interior. This will thus enable us to learn all about the land. At the same time we must survey the island, so as to learn its extent, as well as its general shape and outline."

"But how can we survey it without the instruments?"

"That is readily done, by observing the headlands, or some special coast line marks, and then taking the angles from those points."

"Well, that will be interesting, at least. How shall we start?"

"Do you see that point to the south which may be five or ten miles away?"

"Yes."

"Now, examine the compass, and turn it so that the cardinal points are directly north and south. Now sight across the face of the compass so that you get the exact line between this point and yonder object. What do you make it to be?"

"Why I make it out to be S. E."

"That is correct. The line 1 is south by east."

"But how can we find out how long line 1 is?" asked Harry.

"Why by triangulation," said George, quickly.

"I know that, but how can we do it on sea?"

"It can be done on sea, as well as on land, but we had better go and make the first measurement by triangulation correctly, and do this in our subsequent measurements, unless it should be necessary to make the measurements at sea. The plan followed on shipboard will be found similar to the plan followed on land."

The boat was manned and the boys with a crew of the men and John made for the shore, and together they went inland to a point marked B (Fig. 5), and sighted across to the same object C that was noted of the ship. This, then, gave three lines, 1, 2 and 3, forming a triangle.

"If these angles are placed on a paper the distance from A to C can be determined on the principles of proportion," remarked John.

"How is that done?"

"We will assume that the lines 1, 2, are at right angles to each other. This is not necessary, but it happens to be so in this case. Let us first measure the distance along the line 2, which may be any number of inches, or feet. Suppose we call the line one inch long. Then draw the line 1, so that it will be sufficiently long to be sure and meet the line 3."

"Yes; I now see how it is done," remarked George, with enthusiasm. "If the line 3 is drawn at the angle we got, when we looked at C, from B, the line will cross line 1 at C."

"That is correct. Now, if it is one inch from A to B, we may use that inch as a measurement to get the distance along the line."

"Let me step it off," said Harry. "I find it is just two and three-quarters inches."

"What was the distance, in feet from A to B?" asked John.

"I have the figures here," said George. "We found it was six hundred and ninety feet."

"If, now, you will multiply 690 by 2-3/4, we shall have the distance from this point A, and yonder point, or headland C."

"I make it out to be just 1897.5," was Harry's conclusion.

The boys, together with John and a half dozen of the natives, went along the shore, and mounted the point C, and from that place selected another point in a southerly direction, and again made the same calculations.

The vessel in the meantime was put under sail and anchored

a mile below, giving the surveying party time to make several triangulations, and late in the afternoon the party came on board, tired and ready to take a rest.

From the position taken up by the ship they could see a long stretch of shore line, practically straight, trending toward the southeast, and with their glass could see, miles away, a headland which afforded a pronounced point for observation.

The next morning the same parties rowed to the shore, and Uraso was left with the party to guard the shore boat, while Muro accompanied John and the boys. On this occasion John issued the following instruction:

"The long point which you see in the distance is, probably, 15 miles beyond. It is not more than that, but this clear atmosphere is liable to deceive. I have instructed Sutoto to wait until one o'clock today, and if by that time there is no word from us Uraso will return to the ship, and you will take up anchor and steer for the headland beyond."

"So that you may understand our movements, we will strike into the interior, taking a course due east, for ten miles, or thereabout, and then turn to the south, and reach the sea near the place where the vessel will be located."

"I understand, now, how the distance can be measured by triangulation on land; but how to get the distances, on shipboard, is what puzzles me," said Harry.

John smiled as he replied: "I knew you would come to that sooner or later, so I prepared a little sketch (Fig. 7), which shows the bow of a vessel, and the tall mast. The lines from A to B give an angle with the vertical line of the mast, which will enable you to determine how far the ship is from any point."

"But I am still in the dark as to how, even if we have that distance, we can thereby tell by triangulation, on the vessel, how far one point is from another on the land."

"After the distance from the vessel to the point is determined, as I have shown, then the length of the ship itself is used as the two points to sight from, and the two lines thus projected, from the opposite ends of the vessel, together with the line lengthwise along the ship, form a triangle, the same as the triangle lines 1, 2, 3."

It might be well at this place to describe the equipment of the party as it left the boat. The natives carried a plentiful supply of provisions. Each had a gun, the best kind of breech loaders, and also a spear.

The natives love to handle spears better than anything else in the way of a weapon, and each also had a knife, and some carried the inevitable bolo, that primitive form of hatchet which is known all over the world where steel or iron is available, and the people have arrived at such a state that they are able to make metal articles.

John and the boys also carried guns, but the boys had revolvers, seven shooters, not of large bore, but very convenient weapons, in close quarters. Each carried also a knife, and belt to contain the cartridges for the guns.

Harry carried a camera, which he had brought from the States, and George had the field glass strapped across the shoulders. John felt that they had a force large enough to make a fairly effective stand against a pretty strong force of natives, the entire party counting, in this instance, sixteen.

As they advanced into the interior, it was evident that they were gradually ascending, so that at about six miles from the landing place they reached the crest of the rising ground. Beyond, where the nature of the ground permitted they saw clearly that the distance beyond had a lower altitude than the place where they stood.

During this trip there was no evidence that the island was occupied, but they saw the most amazing evidences of tropical fruits and trees. Magnificent trees were in evidence everywhere, and the woods, besides mahogany, and ebony, were of the most valuable character.

John noted all these things, but the boys were most interested in the birds and animals which roamed about. The latter were not large or vicious looking, but it was not permitted to shoot any of them lest it might alarm Uraso, who was at the landing.

Ahead could be seen several ridges, one of them heavily wooded. Reaching the summit they beheld a beautiful valley below, and opposite on a shelving rock, stood a type of mountain deer like a sentinel, while a dozen or more were feeding on the green slope beneath.

Frequently on the march the boys would take side trips, in the attempt to run down some of the curious animals, but they were careful to keep the main force in sight.

Thus they tramped on fully five miles beyond the crest of the ridge, and occasionally John would stop to examine some suspicious-looking indication of habitation.

"It would surprise me very much to find that the island is not inhabited," he said, as he examined what appeared to be a path.

At this juncture one of the native scouts came up and showed

John a curious stone formation. John took it, and turned it over several times. "That is part of a stone hatchet." The scout nodded assent with a smile.

All now became intent on searching. This finally resulted in bringing to light a well-formed spear, not unlike those originally used on Wonder Island among the native tribes.

Surely they were getting evidence pretty fast now. Then, while crossing a little rivulet, one of the scouts plainly saw the print of a native foot, which was unmistakable. True, it had been made days before, probably a month, but there it was, and now it was incumbent on them to find out where the people were.

The entire party scattered along the little stream, and searched both banks for a considerable distance, the boys taking an active part in the work. Usually the boys kept together, and entertained each other, but on this occasion all were so intent on discovering where, and in what direction the footprints would lead, that they quite forgot to watch each other.

John gave a customary whistle, as he was in the habit of doing, when it was desired to call the party together, and all of the scouts promptly returned, as well as Harry. George was nowhere to be seen. John questioned Harry. He had first missed him at the bend in the stream not two hundred feet to the north.

He rushed back in that direction, while John gave another blast on the whistle, and then listened intently for a reply. Harry came back without any intelligence, and almost frantic. John and the scouts then broke into a run, and Harry turned with them.

That instant a shot rang out. "That must be George," exclaimed John. "Forward as quickly as possible."

The party turned the bend of the river. All along this part of the stream the banks were cut up by ridges and diminutive cliffs, and in many places were large shelving rocks which came up close to the stream.

Immediately after the shot John stopped, and listened for some sound, and the natives, usually so alert to recognize noises, did likewise.

"That shot means that George is in some danger," said John.

"But why does he not answer the whistle? Why should he shoot, and then not call to us, if there is any danger," said Harry in despair.

They turned the bend, and searched to and fro. The shot could not have been more than eight hundred feet away. The searchers spread out into a fan-shaped formation. One of the scouts ran up hurriedly and called to John, who went forward, and there, alongside of a huge rock, where there was little grass, he saw unmistakable evidence of a scuffle.

"These are the footprints of George's shoes," remarked Harry.

"Yes, and here are the prints of the native feet," said John, as one of the scouts distinctly pointed out two or three well defined marks.

"They are, undoubtedly, near at hand. We must now be on our guard," said John, as he pondered on the situation.

"I wonder why they didn't attack us?" asked Harry.

"The reason, no doubt, is that it is a small party. A larger body would not have attempted to capture one of us by stealth."

John turned to Hasmo, one of the fleetest runners, and instructed him to go back to the landing place at once, and advise Uraso to bring his men and provisions, as well as additional ammunition, and to hold the ship until additional word should be sent.

Hasmo was off in an instant, and then John issued additional instructions. "It is evident," he said, "that we must look for the people to the east or, more likely, toward the southeast. That is the reason why I had the boat held at the place where we have just landed. There is also another reason why I think the tribes, if there are any, are to the south, and that is, in this latitude they are much less exposed to the effects of the great winds that occur at certain portions of the year."

Harry wandered about, not knowing what to do, at this terrible catastrophe. George in the hands of the savages! He could hardly believe it.

"Don't worry about George too much," said John consolingly. "I am inclined to think he has had enough experience within the past two years to help him out of immediate trouble, and we will then be able to take a hand."

This somewhat relieved Harry. It is possible that George might be able to take care of himself. "But suppose they kill him?" This was his great fear.

"It is not at all likely they will do that," remarked Muro. "Those who captured him form only a small party, and it is not at all likely that there was a chief with them. Under the circumstances they would not dare kill him until the Chief ordered it."

John smiled as he nodded at the explanation given by Muro. After all, it was not as bad as it might be. Now to the rescue. Muro begged permission to do scouting work until Uraso arrived, and selecting Stut as his companion, they glided through the forest directly to the east.

They were now fully twelve miles from the boat, and the runner could be depended on to reach Uraso within an hour, if not hindered on the journey. It would then take, possibly, two hours more for the party to return, so that it was safe to assume that they would have to remain in the vicinity for the next three hours.

John decided that the time should be spent in exploring the directions to the southeast and to the northeast as well, so they might be well informed when the reinforcements arrived.

Hasmo glided through the forest like a deer. He knew that it was imperative to reach the shore before one o'clock, because at that time the vessel would leave for the southeastern point. To get there too late would mean a trip for fifteen miles or more along the shore to reach the next landing.

The dense forest near the shore prevented him from seeing the vessel until he crossed the last ridge, and when he finally came within view of the harbor the ship had disappeared. He stopped and glanced to the south, but no ship was in sight. This was a situation which had been considered, from the point of view of the departure of the vessel; but where had it gone?

He went to the shore, where Uraso's party had been, and then, laboriously ascended the point beyond, and from which he could get a clear view of the sea. There, far beyond, was the *Pioneer*, sailing to the southeast under a strong breeze.

He tore off his jacket, and seizing a branch, began to wave it back and forth. The ship went on, and there was no indication that they noticed him. He remained thus for nearly a quarter of an hour, and then knew that he must follow the ship until he reached the next landing place.

The trip along the shore was a most difficult one, as he could not follow the beach. Many of the rocks along the shore were licked by the waves, so that he had to take a course beyond the cliffs, and the land was not only rough, but numerous gulleys, or draws, as they are called, were washed out, making speed impossible.

It required more than two hours to make the trip, and it was considerably after three when he hailed the boat from the shore, and hurriedly told the story of George's capture.

Uraso was not slow in gathering the men needed for the expedition, and when the guns and ammunition were brought out all of the men actually begged to go along, but he knew that John would not sanction leaving the vessel without a crew.

*   *   *   *   *

John and his scouts impatiently awaited the return of the men and during this time received the reports from the scouts as they came in. It was evident from the slight traces found that the band which captured George had gone east. It was no doubt from some indication to this effect obtained by Muro, that induced him to take his course in that direction, also.

All had departed but Muro: Four o'clock came, and then five, but neither Muro nor Uraso appeared. This did, indeed, look strange to John, who could, in a measure, account for Muro's non-appearance; but he could not understand why Uraso did not come. It then occurred that after all Hasmo might not have been able to reach the landing before sailing time, and with this theory he consoled Harry, who was constantly on the alert, waiting for tidings.

CHAPTER VII

CAPTURE OF GEORGE BY THE NATIVES

Let us now follow George. He went along the stream on its westerly side, while Harry was examining the eastern shore. Coming to a little rivulet, which flowed into the main stream at this point, he passed alongside the projecting ledges of rock, that for the moment hid him from the view of Harry.

Here he saw some peculiar rocks, and outcroppings, which reminded him so forcibly of the early days on Wonder Island, when the Professor so strongly impressed on them the value of investigation. The gun was stood up, leaning against the rocks, when he was seized by two strong arms, and a hand placed over his mouth.

In the struggle his hand touched the gun, and as his captor drew him back, he took the gun with him, and no effort was made to dispossess him of the weapon. He was carried along, one hand pinioned to his side, while the other hand carrying the gun was free, but he was unable to use it.

He could not have been carried more than a hundred feet, before he heard John's whistle. This startled his captors, for he now saw that there were two burly specimens, almost wholly naked, and for the moment the hold on the imprisoned arm was relaxed.

Quick as a flash he drew up the gun and fired. This was the shot heard by John and Harry. The shot was such a surprise that the savages were almost paralyzed, and dropped their hold, but it was only for an instant. Realizing that the noise was made by George's weapon, and not caused by any of the boy's companions, the nearest savage swung around viciously, and poor George was knocked unconscious by the blow.

How long he remained in this state he did not know. When consciousness returned he was lying, on some tufted grass, and a half dozen vicious looking savages stood around him. Then he remembered the circumstances of his capture.

He eyed them for a time, and then slowly sat up. One of the party had George's field glasses slung around him, just as he himself had them on when captured. One of them was fondling the gun, but it was evident from the manner in which he held it that he had no knowledge of its uses.

His cartridge belt graced the form of one of the other savages, and it was evident that they considered the things thus taken more in the nature of ornaments than as weapons. He slowly felt his pockets and was surprised that they had removed nothing.

While he was rising to a sitting posture he could feel his revolver, and wondered why he had not been disarmed. A glimmer of joy shot through him. His hands were free, and he had no pain, except the sore feeling that was keen on the side of his head, and which was, no doubt, caused by the blow.

Not a word was spoken by either. He hoped something

would be said and probably he would be able to recognize the language, as his two years' experience in Wonder Island gave him a fairly good understanding of the native tongues.

He pronounced some words, in the Saboro and also in the Illya dialect, but they stared at each other, and answered in some words that were utterly unlike anything known on their own island.

Soon, after a conversation among themselves, he was raised up and urged forward. The first thing that George did was to note the position of the sun, and he then stealthily drew out his watch.

When the savages, who were closely watching him, saw the watch two of them pounced upon him, and in the struggle, one of them tore it from the chain. The holder of the chain threw it away, and attacked the one who had the watch.

This was certainly an interesting struggle for George to witness. He had his thoughts, however. Now was the time to make a strike for liberty, so he quietly moved his hand toward the revolver. George was not aware that a pair of eyes was intently watching him while the struggle was going on.

Before the hand reached the revolver, the savage leaped forward. His heart sank. The opportunity was lost. He dove down into the pocket and brought forth a knife, and it was hardly out of his pocket until the prying native had it in his hand.

George gave a forced smile. The native saw it, and looked admiringly at the beautiful handle. He turned it around and viewed it from every side, and then deftly drew a strand of material from his clout and, winding it around the knife, threw the loop of the strand over his head.

This, too, then, was an ornament! They did not know the uses of the knife. George kept up the smile, and soon the savage smiled in return. This was a good beginning, surely! But what surprised him most of all was the perfectly natural manner in which the defeated party in the contest after the watch took his loss.

The victor fashioned it as a pendant, and the other looked calmly on while his opponent admired it. There was not a particle of resentment in the loser.

George did not show any alarm to the savages, although it would be too much to say that he was entirely at ease. The instructions received from John, the experiences of Tom and Ralph when they were captured, were lessons for him, so, when the savages smiled back at him he pointed to the knife, and made motions as though he intended to open the blade.

All savages are curious. Many of them have this trait developed to a remarkable degree. George's motions attracted the man. Then he leaned forward, and removed the knife from the loop. He held it up, exactly like a magician would exhibit some article that he intended should disappear.

Then, as the savage's mouth was now open, he inserted his thumb nail into the crease of the large knife, and opened the blade. Then he extended out his hand, and offered the open knife to the savage.

To say that he was merely surprised is putting it mildly. He could not possibly open his eyes wider, and instead of taking it, drew back. Then George quickly closed the blade again, and offered it in that way, and he was induced to slowly take it back, while he glanced at George suspiciously.

The burly individual who carried the field glass was then approached by George. The latter took the glasses and put them to his eyes. At this act the savages set up a whoop, and the glass was snatched from him. Evidently they thought it was something like the gun.

George smiled, and again made the motion, as though he desired to take the glass. The savage took the loop from his neck, and handed the instrument to George. The latter put it to his eyes and pointed them to the east, carefully adjusting them to get the proper focus.

To his surprise he saw the evidences of a village in the far distant landscape, and, beyond it, the sea. What a discovery this was, indeed!

The glasses were then presented to the burly savage, who now claimed its ownership, and tried to induce him to look through it. In this George finally succeeded, and after he saw the effect of the distant landscape, the attitude of the man changed, and he looked on George with a species of admiration and wonderment.

George walked about them, in the most careless manner imaginable, but they never took their eyes from him. He smiled at them, again took the knife and performed the feat over and over again, and then instructed the savage how to do it.

Suddenly he thought of the match safe. What a jolly trick that would be to spring on them. But it would be more effective at night, he reflected, and so he refrained from taking it out. It was evident, however, that he was making a hit of some kind. Whether it would aid him in escaping he did not know, but he tried every means possible to ingratiate himself, and to show that he had no fear. The view of the village which he had accidentally discovered impressed itself on him with startling force. If he once reached the village escape would be difficult, and consequently he viewed the searching eyes of his captors with great uneasiness.

This was evident by the cat-like action of the one who got the knife. If he made the slightest move of his hands, he could see the eyes following them. Once he stumbled as they were marching along. This was purposely done, in the hope that during the time he was recovering his erect position he could draw the revolver.

He had his course of action all planned out. He had no desire to kill, and he made up his mind that he would first cover them and then by motions wave them away, but it would be necessary to depend upon mimicry for this.

He had learned from John that savages are naturally the most expert pantomimists, and are able to express many things by gestures, this faculty having been made the more acute because the different tribes are frequently brought into contact without any connecting link in the dialects or languages.

If they refused, or made any attempt to seize him, he would then shoot the leader, and thus strike terror into the others. But while he was thus arranging all the details in his mind, he was startled at seeing a whole group of savages leap from the side of the ill-defined path, which they were now traveling, and they speedily surrounded the captor and captive.

Then began a bedlam of explanations as they crowded around George. Some came up and felt his arms, and other portions of his body. He smiled meanwhile. It was the only thing he could do, and he knew it would be useless to look troubled.

The next moment the visitors were examining the glass, the cartridge belt, the knife and the watch, and George was, temporarily forgotten, although surrounded so that he could not possibly force his way through.

He thought it a remarkable thing that they should thus hold and watch him with such tenacity. While thus discussing him, a new party appeared, and now for the first time there was an attempt to show deference.

The leader of the party was the most powerful savage George had ever seen. Uraso was a powerful warrior, and Chum was also noted for his strength, but it seemed that the man now coming up must be a giant. Some of the immediate party rushed up to him, and after making a respectful bow, told him of the capture.

He approached with dignity, and those around George moved away.

Without a moment's hesitation George moved toward the Chief, and when ten feet away, he stopped, straightened himself erect, and with a most courtly bow smiled as he recovered his position.

The strong and resolute manner in which this was done was really a cause for marvel in the savage. He looked at his people, and spoke a few words, and those who had been his guards came forward most deferentially, and, so far as George could understand, told of the circumstances surrounding his capture.

But there was one thing which struck George as a peculiar thing. The three men who had participated in the loot of his valuables did not exhibit them while talking to the Chief.

There was a long palaver, and many gestures indulged in. The question occurred to him: What had become of the articles which they had taken? Did they purposely hide them?

At the close of the conversation two of the Chief's immediate associates came forward, and began to investigate his belongings. The first thing they brought out was the revolver, and at this George was almost on the point of breaking down. Then he grew bitter.

The silver match box was the next to attract the attention of the searchers; and so they went through from one pocket to the other in the most approved style.

These were laid before the Chief who grunted his approval at the different things, and his admiration, judging from the character of his remarks, was unbounded at the silver-plated revolver.

From the curious way in which he handled it George was alarmed. It was an automatic, and if the Chief once pulled the trigger there would be trouble for some one. George held up a warning hand, and the Chief looked up from the weapon.

The only thing he could do was to point to the revolver, and vigorously shake his head. The Chief looked around as though inquiring the meaning of such a sign. He was not interfered with as he walked up to the savage, and held out his hand. The Chief handed him the weapon.

Then, picking up a leaf, he motioned to one near him to place it on the side of a tree. At a word from the Chief the man did so, but George motioned to him to carry it still further away. He took deliberate aim, and thanks to his long and regular practice, the leaf received the impress of the bullet, while the savages jumped in all directions at the report.

Only the Chief remained impassive. He never moved, but when the leaf was brought to him, he looked on the youth with a kindly smile. George was quick to notice this. He again walked over to the Chief, and placed the weapon in his hand, and guided his finger to the trigger, while at the same time holding up his hand so as to sight it.

This time the shot was directed to the nearest tree. The savages scurried to give them room. When the Chief pulled the trigger and the discharge followed, George caught him by the arm, and took him to the tree, pointing out the hole made by the bullet.

There was a wondering look on the Chief's face. He looked at the weapon, and then at the hole. There was a question in the peculiar guttural sounds of his language, which slowly came from his lips. Evidently the Chief wanted to know something.

Ah! he knew what it was. What made the hole? George took the weapon, and extracted one of the bullets, and then pointed to the hole in the tree. It was plain that even this did not satisfy him. Better still; why not dig out the bullet; and as he thought of it he instinctively reached in his pocket for the knife.

Then he remembered. One of his captors had it. Without any ceremony he walked over to the man who had it, and by motions indicated that he wanted the knife. The savage was mute. He boldly searched the folds of the rude clout, and without a protest on the part of the savage he brought forth the coveted knife.

This action was indeed a surprise to the Chief. A frown gathered on the Chief's face. George saw it, and really trembled for the first time, as he saw the eyes of the Giant riveted on the knife, and then turned to the culprit. The latter fell to the ground, and muttered something, and instantly the two others were also seized, as they uncovered the other belongings and laid them before the Chief.

George looked on the scene with genuine regret. The culprits were led away, and he speculated on their fate. But the Chief's eyes immediately returned to the hole in the tree, while the gaze of the others rested on the cartridges, the watch and the field glasses. The knife was in George's hand, and he slowly opened it whereat the appearance of the blade startled the Chief. He was all eagerness now, so George closed the blade and opened it again, and then cut a circle around the bullet hole and chipped the wood away.

There was the bullet, and he slowly drew it forth, a shapeless bit of lead. When he had deposited it in the Chief's hand, he laid one of the cartridges alongside, and also showed the empty shell. Then he quietly laid the closed knife in the Chief's hand and stood back with his arms folded, as though he owned the entire Island.

If the action of the Chief counted for anything the boy did have everything in sight. The Chief returned the revolver to George, and then began to examine the articles before him. The most interesting appeared to be the cartridge belt. He looked at the revolver and cartridges, and then turned over the revolver bullet and shell which George had exhibited.

It was now plain that the Chief could not understand the use of the large cartridges. George's mind was working by this time. He did not recall that the gun was in evidence at any time after they met the first crowd on the road.

The Chief pointed to the cartridges, and George looked toward the group which had captured him. This was enough for the wily savage. A stern command was issued, and in an incredible short space of time the gun appeared. Where it could have been hidden was a marvel. Certainly these people must be adepts in the art of concealment.

The Chief handled the gun in a most awkward fashion and George politely took it from his hand, and after glancing about for a moment, saw a bird on a branch. This he brought down, upon which one of the men ran forward, picked it up and brought it to the Chief. After this the weapon was turned over to him, and the peculiar chuckle that followed was, undoubtedly, the savage's way of expressing delight.

One of the attendants then came forward at the order of the Chief, who, after the articles were gathered up, indicated to George that he should follow, and turned toward the village. George did not regard the prerogatives of royalty, but he took up a most democratic position by the side of the Chief, to which the latter did not object.

It required nearly an hour before they reached the village. Women and children, and boys his own age were in evidence everywhere. They came out of the huts and followed the procession, on the way to the Chief's quarters.

Singularly George did not now feel the slightest bit of fear. On the other hand, there was confidence, a sort of assurance that he could not express. This feeling came to him, not so much from the general demeanor of the Chief, as on account of the one act, namely, the return to him of the revolver.

The Chief's home was an entirely different sort of affair from the other dwellings. It was noted that, the homes of the ordinary people were made singularly like those of the tribes on Wonder Island, usually of twigs braided and brought together at the upper end so as to form cone-like enclosures, and all were covered with clay, so as to keep out the rains.

Outside of these houses appeared to be the sleeping quarters, and a glance at some of them impressed George as being exceedingly filthy. The houses were intended only for the rainy season, apparently, as was the custom in many places on their own island.

But the Chief's dwelling was a most pretentious affair, judged by the surrounding homes. It had a large interior court, without a roof, but the immediate dwelling had four or more rooms. The Chief walked through one room, and entered the court, where George was embarrassed to see two girls, and several boys, together with three women, all of whom stared at him, the girls giggling exactly as he had seen them do at home.

The articles taken from him were then deposited upon the floor, and the Chief reclined on a sort of raised couch. George glanced around and the first thing that his eyes met was a chair, in one corner of the room, and then some articles that he knew could not have been made on the island.

This was his introduction to the home of the Chief. He then fell to wondering how it would be possible to talk and tell him about his friends.

CHAPTER VIII

FIGHT OF THE NATIVES FOR THE TRINKETS

Scouting in an unknown country, with assurances that foes may be in ambush at every turn, is not a rapid way of marching. Ordinarily, in the open road, a man will walk three or four miles an hour. But in a forest, where every tree may conceal a foe, it is quite different.

Muro was an expert in scouting work. He had had years of experience in this sort of life, and, moreover, was a chief of one of the most powerful tribes on the island.

He and his companion went directly east, in the most stealthy fashion, and, a half mile beyond they circled to the south, next swinging around to the north, so as to take in as wide a sweep as possible.

Before dark they obtained the first real traces of the tramp of feet, and as it was now too late to enable them to follow up the trail they went back toward the scene of the capture, so that they might thus be able to follow the trail easily the next morning.

It was very dark when they crept in and were halted by the sentries which John had posted. Harry was the first to greet

Muro. "Have you found anything?"

"Yes," answered Muro. "We know the direction they have gone. In the morning we can go on from the place where we discovered the trail."

"How far is it from here?"

"More than ten miles."

The distance mentioned was in itself sufficient evidence that Muro had not wasted time.

They spent the remaining hours of the evening awaiting further news and it was fully ten o'clock before the sentry to the south reported the probable approach of Uraso. Harry leaped out from the circle, and followed the sentry. It was, indeed, Uraso who had been reporter.

"Tell me all about it," he requested, and Harry, with a voice full of pathos, told him how it happened. When he had finished, Uraso said:

"I was told by my father that somewhere here in the seas was an island where were found most terrible people, who killed every one they captured. I hope this is not the place." And Uraso did not say this to excite Harry's fears, but, like many natives, he was frank, and open in his speech.

"I hope there will be no trouble," was Harry's response.

"We need not worry about George," added Uraso. "The way that he was taken shows that they are taking him to the Chief. A boy like George would be likely to interest the Chief, at first for a time, and time is all we want."

"I am glad you have the same opinion as John," answered Harry.

John, Muro and Uraso held a conference that night. As a result Harry was comforted to know and feel that George was safe, and that within a day or two at most, they would be able to come up with the tribe.

The entire party now numbered thirty-five, all well armed. In the morning, as soon as it was light enough to see they were up, and after a quick breakfast Muro directed them along the trail made the night before, and the spot where Muro found the trace was reached about nine o'clock.

John and his party now spread out so as to take in a wide expanse, and they marched toward the east for fully two hours. Sometimes all traces would be lost, and then there would be a halt and a search, and the native wit of the scouts was generally acute enough to recover the trail.

During these periodical searches, one of the men bounded forward with a cry, as he held up a hand in which something was swinging.

As usual Harry was there like a shot. "That is George's chain," he cried out.

"Where did you find this?" asked John.

The scout rushed over to the place, and all followed. The ground about plainly showed the evidences of the struggle where George's captors fought for the possession of the watch.

The trail was beginning to get warm. It was readily followed for several miles, and then disappeared, but after patient hunting it came to light, and shortly after noon the spot was reached where the Chief came on the scene, and the appearance of the ground indicated that there must have been a large number in the party.

Here was an occasion where one great quality of many savage tribes stands out so prominently, and that is in determining the number of their enemies by the foot prints. Hundreds of imprints on the soil, crossing and recrossing each other, will to the untrained seem a hopeless riddle.

On one occasion on Wonder Island, John stated that one of a party they were trailing, was wounded in one of his legs. The explanation was simple: The pressure of the foot in the soil was less on the lame than on the sound leg, and the stride was uneven.

But the scouts had to decipher the peculiar imprint of each foot, and then compare it with all the others, in turn.

"I could tell the difference in the shape of a shoe from another," said Harry, "but I do not see how it is possible to tell one foot print from another."

"How do you distinguish people?" asked John.

"Well, usually, by their faces."

"Quite true. Now feet are just as different as faces are. But there are other ways by which we recognize people."

"Yes," was the response. "I can tell who many people are at distances so great that I cannot see their faces."

"How do you do that?"

"By the way they walk, by their size, or by some action that seems to be peculiar to them."

"The observations are correct," answered John. "At the same time, if all the men you knew happened to be in a crowd, and moving around among each other, you would be able to recognize and place each without any difficulty; is not that true!"

"Yes; and I think I understand the trend of your remark now."

"And what is that?"

"You mean to say that if the scouts are able to read, or to become acquainted with the foot prints, they can read them as readily as I would read the faces of my friends."

"That is the exact inference I wish to draw."

"Well, I want to see that done," and Harry followed up Uraso, and watched Muro, and the most intelligent of the scouts, while they carefully stepped over the ground, each being careful while doing so to step in the foot marks of the preceding scout.

"That is a curious thing to do," he remarked, as he turned to John.

"What is that?" the latter asked.

"Stepping in the tracks made by the leader."

"That is for the purpose of keeping the surface of the ground absolutely the same as the tribe left it."

"Well the boys seem to understand detective work pretty well."

All of them laughed at this complimentary allusion, as it must be understood that all the scouts taken from the island had learned to speak the English language, and some of them, like Uraso, were exceptionally skilled.

When the different ones had gone over the ground thoroughly, John asked the opinion of the searchers.

"From my count there must have been twenty-four," remarked Uraso.

Muro smiled, as he said: "Uraso is mistaken, there are twenty-five." Uraso was not at all perturbed, but walked over to the surveyed plot and said: "The most prominent one is the fellow with the spreading toes. See! here is his left foot. See that broad foot is all around the place. This broad foot with a toe missing, is another fellow; and here are two with rather long feet, you can see them all about, and they are, no doubt, active fellows."

"Well, that is picking them out plainly enough," remarked Harry.

"But," continued Uraso, "I want you to look at this foot. It is the largest I ever saw."

"I am satisfied that fellow is the Chief," remarked Muro.

"There is evidence of that here too," said Uraso, as Muro nodded his head.

Harry looked on in bewilderment. "Assuredly that is something new. How do you know *that*?" he asked.

"The best indication is," said Uraso, "that the fellow with the big feet does very little walking, and all the other fellows have danced about him."

Harry laughed, and was satisfied. "That was certainly clever," he remarked. "But why shouldn't they be clever. These boys are the finest and bravest in the world," and Uraso and Muro smiled and were happy at this encomium of the boy they all loved so much.

"The last foot I have counted is that little sawed-off sample that has danced all around the edge; see it here, and here!"

Muro walked forward, and, stooping down, pointed to the imprint of a shoe, said: "That is our boy's shoe."

Uraso laughed, as he admitted neglecting George's presence in the crowd of prints. "But I have found something else. George has had an interview with the Chief. He has been making some explanations to the Chief about his revolver."

John smiled, and kept his eye on a tree to the right.

"And how do you know that?" asked Harry.

Uraso walked over to the tree, after picking up something, and pointed to a cut-out in the side of the tree. It was the mark of the bullet, and the circular cut which George had made that John had observed, and which had been noticed by Uraso and Muro.

"The scene here looks very promising to me," said John.

"Yes, it is better and better," remarked Muro.

"But you haven't told us yet, how you know that George was

interviewing the Chief."

"Come here and I will show you. Now look closely at the foot prints of George. Then observe the indications as to the attitude of the Chief. George goes up to the Chief. They turn around. Here is a shell. Beyond is the tree where they had the mark, and here are the tracks of the Chief and George as they go up to the tree."

Harry was now convinced. It must be said, however, that many of the marks made were so illy-defined, that it required extraordinary vision to observe them, and this is what Harry marveled at.

"What you say only proves the value of minute observation," remarked John. "Those who are not accustomed to see these things, can not detect what are very plain markings. Sometimes a slightly torn leaf, under certain conditions, will tell a story in itself,—just such a commonplace and ordinary thing as a ruptured leaf."

The consensus of opinion was that there were fully twenty-five in the party counting George, and it is remarkable that when the matter was afterwards investigated it was found that Uraso's count was right.

There were six in the party which took George, twelve who surrounded the party before the Chief arrived, and five more were with him when he came up.

Another consultation was held. John remarked: "I am of the opinion that the people who have captured George are not at all bad, or vindictive. Therefore we must exercise care and not needlessly injure any of them. I need not say that it is our purpose here to aid the people, to make friends of them, and not enemies."

"That is in accordance with our wish," said Uraso, with the approval of all present.

"It is perfectly evident that these people, in taking George, did what most people in a savage condition would do. The great and overshadowing trait in humanity is to acquire something. It is just possible that the cartridge belt, or the field glasses, or the buttons on his coat were of more importance to them than George himself."

"Then you mean they had to get George to get the buttons," said Harry, laughing in his relief.

"Of course," answered John, and Muro laughed aloud, as he recalled his first experiences with the boys.

"John has hit upon the very thing which is at the bottom of the whole business. All we wanted was to get the trinket, and the prisoner belonged to the Chief."

"Or to the Krishnos," remarked Muro.

"Well we might as well go on if we can find the trail," remarked John.

"Yes, it is plain enough now," answered one of them.

"But let us exercise caution," remarked John. "Move along slowly and keep a sharp lookout on our flanks."

Harry was walking by the side of Uraso. There had always been a warm friendship between the two. Lolo, Uraso's favorite son, was Harry's age, and the two were companions, and this was a source of great joy to the Chief, for Uraso was the head man of the Osagas, and one of the most progressive of all the prominent men.

Harry was dangling the chain which had been found in the morning. "I have been wondering why he dropped this!" he asked.

"I have an idea that it was lost in the fight for the possession of the watch."

"The fight? Why did they have a fight?"

"Well, the ground where the chain was found looked very much like it."

"I don't see why the fellows don't agree to divide up things properly when they get them, instead of scrambling for them in that way!"

"You can see it is perfectly natural for them to fight for it under the circumstances. They do not understand anything but power."

"I should think the loser would be resentful, and try to even it up on the other fellow," remarked Harry.

"On the other hand, the moment the stronger fellow wins, that is the end of the dispute. The best one won. In his creed there is no other argument. That is the savage's religion. You people have told us differently. The Professor has often said: 'There is only this difference between us, with you, might is right; with us right is might.'"

"Well, what do you really think about it now?" asked Harry.

Uraso did not smile, as he remarked somewhat sadly: "It took me a long time to understand that. How could right be might? At first it looked foolish, and Muro and I talked it over many times. Then Oma, and Tastoa and Oroto, the other

Chiefs, spoke to me about it. But while I did not understand it I had faith in the Professor.

"Then we went to Unity, and built the town, and the people began to go there, and when we saw the Professor, and the way he treated every one, never doing a wrong to anybody, we could not believe that he was sane. But everywhere we went we heard people talking about him, and the way he acted, and we saw all the white people do the same as the Professor did, we noticed that no one would dare say a word against the Professor, or John.

"We marveled at that. The Professor went out among the people of all the tribes, and never carried a weapon of any kind. But no one would have dared to injure him. If a man had even attempted to injure him the people would have torn him to pieces. Then I understood. Right was and is *Might*, but it takes a savage a long time to understand it, and he must learn it from something practical that comes to him in every day life; he will never know it in any other way."

Harry walked on in silence.

CHAPTER IX

THE GIANT CHIEF AND HIS "PALACE"

We must now return to George and see how he fared during the first night of his captivity. After the Chief had seated himself, and had begun to examine the articles taken from George, the latter had an opportunity to examine the surroundings more closely.

The Chief made no remarks to him, nor did he ask him to be seated. At the moment he entered the room he noticed the chair. As the Chief did not pay any attention to him after they entered, George walked over and deliberately sat down on it.

The two attendants who carried in the articles, stared at him, and the women and children, particularly the latter, seemed to be paralyzed at his attitude seated in the chair. It was covered with dust, an evidence that it was never used for the purposes of a seat. On reflection, he thought that must be the reason they looked at him so queerly.

The Chief, however, gave no indication that his act was a rude or questionable one. He tried on the cartridge belt, but it was far too short for his corpulent body, and George could hardly repress a laugh, as he noticed the attempt to adjust it.

The field glasses came in for a share of attention, then the silver match box, and the women craned their heads forward, as it glittered. The Chief held it off from his eyes, so he could properly view it; just as George had often seen women do in trying to match articles.

All the while the Chief was emitting grunts betokening pleasure and satisfaction. The adjusting screw on the field glass next attracted his attention. The turning moved the barrels in and out, and this was, in all probability, the most remarkable thing he ever saw.

George could stand it no longer. He left his seat, the younger children shrinking back as he arose, and quietly walked to the Chief, and sat down in front of him. As he did so he pointed to the match safe which the Chief held in his left hand.

The latter did not resist the attempt to take it, but looked on wonderingly as George pressed the point, and the lid flew open. Then, taking one of the matches from the receptacle, he held the box in one hand, exhibited the match in the other, for a moment, and then drew the match across the box, and ignited it.

The Chief actually drew in a breath that was audible everywhere in that neighborhood. He nodded with approval. Harry closed the box and handed it back; he then directed the Chief's attention to the little point, and pressed it, when the lid again flew open.

This time the Chief closed it, and he pressed the point. The success of the experiment was so great that he eventually called his wife to witness it, for she came over, while he performed the miraculous thing.

He took out a match. Its use was just as great a mystery. He was taught just what to do, and the primitive man sat there and struck the matches, one after the other, in the greatest delight. What amused George more than anything else was, that every time a match was struck, he closed the box, and then opened it before extracting another.

George noted the imitative quality so marked in all savages. It did not, apparently, occur to him that he could strike two matches without the lid flying open in the period intervening the two operations.

It was now growing dark, and soon an attendant came in with several curiously-arranged lights, made from some sort of weed or vegetation, the smoke of which appeared to be most agreeable. From an adjoining room, an appetizing odor reached George and, staring in that direction, the Chief noticed the boy's expectant attitude.

The Chief arose, his mighty frame towering above the rest, and a command was given. Almost immediately two servitors came through the opening, one of them carrying a large bowl of the most savory stew. The bowl was not of native manufacture, and George, observing this, suddenly remembered what John had said, that the Chief was always sure to get the best and most valuable parts of the wreckages along the shore, and he felt sure that this was salvage from some shipwreck.

The Chief smiled, as the bowl was set before him. It was smoking hot, and George smiled back as he noticed the friendly look, and saw that the Chief's wife graciously arranged the accompanying vegetables, although he had no idea what the latter were.

A second attendant brought pointed sticks, and two

paddle-shaped blades. The Chief without ceremony dived into the mess and speared a piece of the meat, and waved it to and fro, to cool it. Here was an opportunity to follow the example thus set, and George was glad to take the hint.

He didn't look around to inquire for a plate, nor did he ask for a napkin. The meat was good, the vegetables appetizing, and the conversation lagged so much that there was no chance for unseasonable interruptions during the meal.

If George had never before that hour witnessed a savage eat, he would have been mortified at the small amount he himself was capable of putting away, when he compared the relative amounts consumed. He was of the opinion, before they began, that the bowl was intended for the whole family, but the Chief ate all of it, except the small part that George disposed of in the meantime.

But he was perfectly content. He ate until he could eat no more, and then to his extreme disgust, a wooden platter of fruit was set before them. Bananas were the only things he recognized. A small pear-shaped fruit attracted him, and then an egg-shaped, brown-colored fruit, with a sweet, strong perfume, was among the varieties.

The Chief was graciousness itself, exhibiting not one trait of selfishness, as he forced the fruit on George. When the Chief had finished the fruit George was relieved, but uncomfortable. He had eaten beyond his capacity. The articles containing the food were removed, and the Chief, who, during this time, was in a reclining position, slowly sank down, and was soon asleep.

The family sat around for a time, and then all slowly disappeared and he could hear the jumble of voices in the adjoining apartment, as they were undoubtedly engaged in their meal.

What a peculiar position to be placed in. Alone with the sleeping savage! Still, he did not seem to be so very savage. There was no one in sight. He arose and walked toward the opening. Not even a guard prevented him from leaving.

He stepped out. He still had his revolver, but that was all. Now was the time to effect his escape. He turned the corner of the main structure, and there stood one of the Chief's girls, the one who had attracted George's attention when he was first ushered into the palace, as George named the place in his mind.

As this girl will have an important place in reciting this history, it may be well to describe her. She was about the height of George, with a much lighter skin than the majority of those whom he had seen thus far. Her eyes were large and beautiful, and while her hair, intensely black and very profuse, was not at all kinky. It should be said that the savages on the island, like those on Wonder Island, while dark, did not have curly hair of the Ethiopian, so that they were not of the negroid type but more nearly allied to the Malay family.

She smiled, and George, abashed for the moment, went up to her, and she did not at all shrink from him. Now that he had made the advance he was at a loss what to do. The only thing that both perfectly understood, was to smile, and smile they did.

But why not say something. He tried it, and those great eyes appeared to open still wider. George turned and waved his hand, and affrighted, apparently, she darted into the side entrance. The darkness prevented him from seeing what was there, and he dared not enter. The moon was shining brightly.

The desire to escape again took possession of him. But why try to escape? He felt sure the Chief meant no harm, and then he wandered to the other side of the building, and there lay the great ocean, the shore of which was not a thousand feet away.

He sat down on a log, and pondered and, feeling fatigued from the unusual efforts of the day, he lay down for a nap. How long he remained there it was impossible to tell, for when he awoke, he found himself by the side of the trunk, and near him two of the body guard who accompanied the Chief the day before.

He sat up, rubbed his eyes, arose, and without any suggestion or command on the part of the watchers, marched back to the Chief's palace, and entered the room to see the latter awake and reclining at his place on the floor.

He offered a salutation to George, and the latter smiled and bowed graciously. One of the attendants touched him on the arm, and he was led to a room, adjoining the court; but there was no door, by means of which he could close the room, nor did he discover a window, or anything suggesting an opening at the other side of the apartment.

A delightful odor came from some kind of grass which was piled in one corner. He examined it, and concluded that it had been placed there for his particular benefit. This was indeed a thoughtful thing on the Chief's part. They were making a home for him, that was evident.

But he was too tired to reflect long on these things. Without removing his clothes he threw himself down on the sweet, clean grass, and he knew no more until, when the morning sun flooded the court, he could peer out, and see the family moving to and fro, but the Chief was nowhere in sight.

While they had not ventured to tell him what was just the correct thing to do, he walked out, and then wandered to the open portal at the front. No one seemed to heed him. He walked down toward the ocean, and saw some women carrying water in curiously-shaped gourds.

He followed the path, which led to a spring; delicious, cool and refreshing. Then he bathed his face, and washed his hands. But he missed the soap. He had not, however, forgotten the early days on Wonder Island, when the Professor found the soap tree.

He glanced around. There, sure enough, was the identical bush, and breaking off several twigs, the small branches were crushed up together with the leaves, and with these he returned to the brook and had a good soap wash.

This peculiar action was witnessed by some of the women, and the tale was quickly told, and became current in the village. When George visited the same spot, the bush had entirely disappeared.

The Chief had not returned when he went back, but his breakfast was ready, and the maiden with the great round eyes, and the mother, evidently, waited on him.

George looked toward the Chief's place. She understood, and pointed to the west. He mused awhile. What could she mean! It must not be supposed that during all this time George was not thinking of Harry, and John, and the boys who came over with them on this trip.

They always called each other "boys." All the natives on Wonder Island were boys to them, and it was amusing to hear them say the word in return. They were all boys, Uraso, and Muro, as well; all but the Professor, John and Blakely.

When George went out after breakfast he was surprised to note the absence of the men. No one but women and children were about. Then the truth flashed on him. The Chief had gone out, on hearing of the approach of John and his party.

He rushed out toward the western path that led from the village, and he had not gone three hundred yards before the men, all armed with spears, came back, with the Chief at their head. All were in consternation.

George knew what this meant now. He held up his hand as they hurriedly moved toward him, and pointed to the west. He did this smiling to assure him of the friendly character of the visit. The Chief stopped. George moved through the group and beckoned the Chief to follow.

He hesitated but a moment, and then gave the necessary command. Coming through the forest beyond were John and the "Boys." When they were still too far for hailing distance George raised his hat and waved it.

When John and his party were still a hundred yards away, they stopped at the unusual sight. Meanwhile George and the Chief moved on. Harry could not restrain himself, and broke from the party, in his mad rush to welcome George.

"Bow, Harry; bow; he is a dandy Chief."

Harry obediently made a gracious bow, and the Chief acknowledged the salute.

All that Harry could say, was: "Oh, George!"

John and the company came up, and George rushed to John, as he said: "I have had the nicest time in the world, but I am afraid the Chief does not know whether you are friends or enemies."

John turned to the men, and quietly said: "This man is a friend, and we must treat him as a Chief. All give him a respectful greeting." The Chief stood still, as all the warriors ranged themselves in front and all bowed low, to the obvious relief of the savage.

Then John brought Uraso and Muro forward, and by well timed gestures indicated to the Chief that they were also Chiefs, and he instantly showed that he recognized the pantomimic language, and deferentially bowed, as he had seen George do.

Uraso stepped forward and went up to the burly form, and pressed his nose against his nose. Then, he spoke a few words. The Chief looked at him for a moment, and then answered. Muro was not slow to follow the example, and he also addressed the Chief.

When Uraso turned and took John's hand and in a dialect, which both seemed to understand, he told about John and the boys, the Chief turned to his men and said a dozen words, which were instantly recognized by Uraso and Muro. They smiled.

"What did he say?" asked George.

"He told them to go to the village and prepare food."

All but a half dozen of the immediate followers of the Chief turned and darted back to the village.

"Do you know the Chief's language?" asked Harry, as Uraso gave way to Muro.

"We can understand each other pretty well. There are many words which are the same, but he uses some which are new to me."

"Do you suppose they are the same people as are on our island?"

"I do not know that. We have heard that all the people in the different islands came from the same place, but where we do not know."

Then the boys crowded around George, and insisted on having him tell his story. Did you ever hear a boy tell a thrilling story of his own adventures? Well George was in his heaven of delight as he told of his treatment, and how he had dined with the Chief, and slept in his palace.

"His palace?" queried Harry.

"Yes, palace! It isn't a common house!" And George dilated on it to such an extent that Harry actually grew envious at the big time that George had at their expense.

The party wended its way down the hill, and when the village was reached the sight there astounded George. He had left it a sleepy place. Now all was bustle. Fires were being built; the men and women were busy preparing food. A species of hog, well known on Wonder Island, was being prepared and spitted, and hung over the heated coals.

They saw the favorite native vegetable, the Taro root, and also, to their surprise, an abundance of Uraso's poison bulb, the Amarylla, which he had tried to prepare in stealth after he had been captured, and the telling of which was the occasion of many jokes at the expense of George and Harry.

John, the two boys, together with Uraso and Muro, were ushered into the Chief's house.

"And this is what you call a 'palace'?" remarked Harry.

"Why not?"

"From your description I thought it might be on top of a big hill with graded steps leading up between rows of flowers, and the rooms filled with statuary, with a large fountain playing in the center of a fine banquet hall."

George laughed at the joke. "The trouble with you is that you are not a philosopher, Harry. If you had been as well treated as I have been you would think the same as I do."

John overheard the conversation, and remarked: "I must say that there is more philosophy in that view than even you, George, appreciate."

"Have I said anything unusual?" he asked with a sort of mock gravity.

"Quite so; have you ever heard the saying 'Handsome is, as handsome does'? Well, that is the root of all true actions in life. From the noble manner in which this Chief treated George, giving him the best that he had, and installing him in the finest room in the house, is doing all that any one can do."

"That is the way I really felt about it at the time. I was tired and hungry, and instead of meeting an enemy, I met a friend."

"Do you see, Harry? George did right in calling this a palace. If it so appears in his heart, and he feels that impulse, isn't that just as real as though you see it with your eyes?"

"I didn't think of it in that way," said Harry, apologetically. "I like the old fellow. He is good enough to be a white man."

CHAPTER X

PECULIARITIES OF THE NATIVE TRIBE

Within an hour the feast was ready, and the men in the open were already making merry with the maidens who prepared the meal. George and Harry frequently nudged each other, as they caught the eyes of some of the native boys who were very attentive to the gentler sex.

Within the Chief's dwelling there was the most animated conversation indulged in by the Chief, Uraso and John, and to this number were added the Chief's brother, and a handsome man who was probably one of the Chief's principal advisors. Muro and Uraso were the interpreters.

The latter, by turns, told the Chief where they sailed from, and what their history had been for the past three years. They told about the wonderful Professor, and all concerning John, and what part the two boys had taken in the transformation of the island.

"But where is this wonderful ship?" asked the Chief.

"On the other side of the island," answered Uraso.

"Then why do you not bring it here?"

"We should have done so, but we did not know we had a friend here."

"I want to see the wonderful place you have told me about,—your home, and how you make people happy," said the Chief.

John's face lit up when this was interpreted to him.

"What do your people work at?" the Chief abruptly asked Muro.

"We make many curious things, like the articles you have here," and he pointed to George's belongings, which were still lying about.

The Chief hurriedly gathered them up and handed them to George. The latter, after turning to John, refused to take them, and addressing Uraso, said: "Tell him that I want him to take them, and my gun, as well."

The Chief could not understand this, and at first refused, but John, as well as Uraso, insisted, and the latter said:

"These boys can make these things, and they do not feel that they are sacrificing anything, beyond what it is their duty to do."

The Chief looked doubtfully at the boys, as he remarked: "Do you tell me that these *memees*, (Boys) made these things?"

Uraso and Muro both assured them that such was the case, and added: "And still more wonderful things."

After some conversation Uraso turned to John and said: "The

Chief wishes to send a runner to bring the ship to the harbor here. Hasmo may accompany him."

This arrangement had John's approval, and when Hasmo was advised of the mission, he jumped up with delight, and, together with the Chief's fleetest messenger, speeded off to make the intervening twenty-five miles.

It was not much of a task for the two men. In less than four hours, Sutoto saw two men on the shore, one of them waving a signal that he understood. A boat was put off, and when the runners came aboard, and the news imparted, all on board sprang to their places, the anchor was hurriedly taken up, and the *Pioneer* soon rounded the point, while they all eagerly scanned the shore.

The Chief and his visitors remained in the "palace" for three hours, while the latter told and retold the stories which so much interested the chieftain. Then John began to question him upon matters that more nearly concerned their visit.

"Ask him," he said, "if they have any Krishnos here?"

"He does not know what they are," answered Muro.

"Does he believe in a Great Spirit?"

"No he has never heard anything of that kind."

"Ask him if he knows who makes the rain and the sunshine, and the clouds."

"He says that the questions are surprising to him."

"Has he never thought of those things?"

"No; all he knows is that he lives and that he is a Chief and is the one who must govern the people."

"Does he know why he is the Chief?"

"Yes; because he is stronger than any one else."

"That would certainly make him a Chief," remarked Harry. "I never saw such a big man."

"Do they have any big holes in the ground!"

When the question was asked he waited a moment, and then slowly shook his head.

"They have nothing of that kind to his knowledge."

The countenances of Harry and George fell. John noticed it, and smiled at the disappointment.

"There are no caves around here," said George.

"Are there any mountains on the island?"

"There are high hills."

"Have they any neighbors, or different tribes?"

"Yes; to the north, (pointing in that direction) are some bad people, but they belong to him."

"Why do they not live near to the village!"

"Because they would make the people bad."

"What did they do that was so bad?"

"They stole and lied."

"From whom did they steal?"

"From the Chief."

"Did they steal from each other?"

"No; they could not steal from each other."

At this remark the boys laughed. John began to be interested now in his questionings.

"Do you mean it is not wrong to steal from each other, but only from the Chief?"

He nodded an assent. This was a curious bit of reasoning. It needed some explanation. John continued:

"Why is it wrong to steal from the Chief and not from each other?"

At this question the Chief did not answer as promptly as usual. He weighed the question in his mind. He smiled as though to say: How can it be wrong for people to take things from each other? They do not own anything. No one but the Chief owns things.

His answer, when finally given, was not at all clear, at least so the boys thought.

"The Chief in his wisdom gives to all alike; and when he gives it the property still belongs to him and not the people; but if they take it from the Chief then they are robbers."

"Ask him," said John, "whether, if when he gives anything to one of his people, and it still belongs to him, after he gives it, why it is not stealing from him, if some one takes it away from the one he gave it to?"

The Chief was not at all taken aback at this question. Pointing to the sun, he said:

"That is a great Chief. He gives seed to the people, and they plant it. But the great Chief does not forget it. The seed comes up to see its father. It still belongs to him. When he gives that seed to the people it is for their use. Every one has a right to take it and use it, and it is no crime. But if he takes it away from the Chief, he destroys what belongs to him, and he then does a wrong which must be punished."

"This may not be very clear to you," said John, "but it means that whoever takes it away and destroys it wilfully, is guilty of a crime. Whatever the Great Chief gives willingly, like the fruits of the earth, is intended for all alike, and men should not be called criminals for taking what they need, if they do not wilfully destroy it."

"That is a wonderful idea, when I come to think of it," remarked George. "And to think that a savage could work that out in his mind."

"But there is one thing that looks a little queer to me. He said he did not know or believe in a Great Spirit, and yet he talks of the sun as a Great Spirit," remarked Harry.

"I will put the question to him," said John. "You said that you did not believe in a Great Spirit, but now you speak about the sun as a Great Chief. Do you not believe in him?"

"No; I only know that he is there; I do not believe in him any more than in the carago (moon)."

A great noise was heard outside; the Chief looked up, as an attendant entered. He spoke to Uraso, and the latter turned to John and said:

"Our ship is coming."

This announcement broke up the interview. It was exciting and interesting from first to last, and when they emerged from the dwelling the host and visitors were friends that the future never could sever. It gave a new inspiration to the boys, and it showed them that even a low state of man was capable of expressing things that were worthy of consideration.

The entire village went to the seashore. The inhabitants wondered at the great vessel, and were impressed at the manner in which it was handled.

"I am anxious to see the man who can row such a vessel," said the Chief.

"He is one of the men from our island," answered Muro.

This seemed to be an astonishing thing to him. He had seen vessels before, but in the distance. At long intervals parts of ships had come ashore; but this was the first time that a vessel had ever landed, within his recollection.

As it drew near he marveled at its size. He could see the man at the bow-sprit who was constantly throwing something attached to a line overboard, and then drawing it in again.

He questioned the reason for such a strange action, and was told that the man was trying the depth of the water, so that they might not come too close to the shore, and strike the bottom. Then some of the sailors dropped something overboard, with a great splash, and a huge sail fell down like magic, and the ship still moved toward the shore and turned around.

The Chief was inquisitive concerning every action. Why did the ship act like a human and turn around? He could hardly believe the statement when told that the anchor was a giant claw, and that when it reached the bottom it took hold and had sufficient strength to stop the ship and make it swing around, as he had witnessed.

A boat was lowered, and the last one to descend was Sutoto. Uraso pointed out his figure, and the Chief kept his eyes on him. The first man to leave the boat was Sutoto, and both boys rushed down to meet him. It was the course they always pursued, to be in the lead to welcome anyone.

They led him to the Chief, and he put his great arms about Sutoto, to the latter's great embarrassment. But what affected Sutoto more than anything else, were the eyes of the Chief's daughter, who had acted so shyly to George the night before. From that moment Sutoto saw no one else, and she,—well, Harry and George laughed, and slyly caressed Sutoto, as they saw her admiring glances.

Sutoto was the handsomest native on Wonder Island. He was the brave and fleet runner who undertook the mission to pass through the three savage tribes to carry a message, written on a plaintain leaf by the Professor, to John and the boys while they were surrounded by the hostiles.

The friendship between him and the boys grew stronger and better from that day on. The tribute to him was one which the boys enjoyed for his sake, and because he deserved it.

There was a feast that night, unparalleled in the knowledge

of the boys. It was like going to a new world, and meeting new people. Only one little thing seemed to mar the joyous occasion for the boys for a time. When they were returning from the beach, they saw three of the natives, together with their wives and children, with their hands bound, and in charge of a half dozen warriors.

George recognized the three as his captors. Then was impressed upon him the fact that they were about to pay the penalty for stealing his things and hiding the theft from the Chief. They were to be exiled to the place where the bad people lived.

George hurriedly told Uraso the story of the theft, and begged him to intercede with the Chief. Instantly, when he learned that George requested it, he turned to Uraso, and said: "He may release them."

He rushed up to the now bewildered culprits, in order to sever the bonds, and then recalling that he had given his knife to the Chief, he called to Harry, and together they freed the limbs of the captives and the Chief, with a few words of admonition, dismissed them. The boys never forgot the grateful looks that came from the men and their wives.

When they had departed Muro said: "Under their law the women and children of the culprits are criminals also, and so they were doomed to go together."

It would be a difficult matter to describe the food prepared and eaten at this banquet. Several varieties of fowl, all wild types, and the wild boar, as well as the 'possum, provided the meats. Of course taro and amarylla were the chief vegetables; and of nuts, the well known Brazil species was found everywhere, and to be seen in all dwellings.

The outer portion of the shell of the Brazil nut formed bowls and cups, which the boys early learned to utilize. There were bananas, a species of fig, and loquats.

"What surprises me is that they have no fish, or sea food of any kind," observed Harry.

John mused for a while, and then said: "It is likely that the people here have the same aversion to fish as some natives along the Australian continent, and in the islands near there."

"What is that?" asked George.

"The natives of New Guinea, for instance, worship snakes, lizards, sharks and crocodiles, and there is a strict law among them not to injure anything, of that kind. As a result, they are afraid to eat anything that approaches the shape of these animals."

"Well, if they worship the snakes they must have some kind of religion," ventured Harry.

"Yes; and with them go the witch doctors who practice on the people and charge fees just the same as the physicians do in our country."

"Do they claim there is a Great Spirit, like some of the people here!"

"No; they have a God called Baigona, who lives in the mountains, and instead of being a good God, is a bad one; he has the power to speak without being heard, to strike without being seen, and he loves and hates, just like human beings. He gives the witch doctor the power to do anything, without being wrong, and without being liable to punishment."

"Well, that is a pretty convenient God to have," said Harry, as he mused at the idea.

The peculiar thing about the absence of sea food at the banquet could not be understood, particularly as the natives on Wonder Island were great fish eaters, and were also the bitter enemies of snakes.

"We must consult the Chief about that," said John.

At the first opportunity the subject was brought up, and it was discovered that the people were afraid to eat anything that came from the sea. And then another thing was learned. There were no rivers of any consequence on the island; only a few streams, that were dry most of the year.

"I can understand," said John, "that in such a case you do not have fresh water fish."

The Chief was, in many respects, a remarkable character. Most natives are extremely superstitious, and it is particularly true of those who have a belief in some form of God. While he would marvel at new things they did not occur to him as being the result of some new occult force.

In this respect he differed from the natives of Wonder Island, all of whom believed, more or less, in the tales of the Medicine Men, and of the witch doctors. Old Suros, of the Berees tribe, was the only one who did not believe in the existence of a being who could rule him.

But the Chief had other qualities which were remarkable in a savage, if such he was. He governed according to some law, and yet he did not know what law was. The only thing in that community was the will of that one man.

If he said something, in adjusting any matter, it was always remembered by the people, and that ruling became a guide for them in the future. Take, for instance, the theft of the articles from George. The three who participated in it, knew that it was not wrong, according to the light they had, to take it from George.

Indeed, the Chief had distinctly said that they could not steal from each other, but only from him, hence the theft of the articles which George owned was not a crime. On what ground, then, were they guilty?

George thought he had solved the problem, when discussing the matter with John. "The Chief found them guilty of trying to hide what they had done, and they were caught at it."

"But the Chief was not covetous. He admitted he did not care for the things, and one of the men told Muro that the Chief never took things from his people without paying for them."

"Well, then, he punished them for trying to deceive him."

"There, that is one of the crimes which the Chief referred to. I think he is a wonderful character, and I hope we shall be able to unite him with us."

CHAPTER XI

SUTOTO AND THE CHIEF'S DAUGHTER

It was plain that Sutoto was not the same being. During the three days they remained at the port, and formed the exploring expeditions into the interior, with the co-operation of the Chief, Sutoto did not take a part.

He begged to be allowed to remain near the ship. That was a sly suggestion which John understood. Even though he might have been blind he would have known the true reason, for the boys were continuously joking Sutoto all of which he took good-naturedly, and John often burst out in fits of laughter, as he witnessed Sutoto's discomfiture.

The Chief's name was Beralsee, and the big-eyed maiden was known as Cinda, the meaning of which, as explained by Beralsee, the Beautiful Star. The Chief had four other children, one a man of twenty-one, and the others younger than Cinda.

The eldest, Calmo, was tall and lithe, like Sutoto. Like his father he was original in his ways, and to him the Chief entrusted the care of the expeditions which were made at the suggestion of John. The latter explained that they had seen the wonderful products growing on the island, coffee, cocoa, spices, and particularly the various fibres.

The recital of the tales, of how the white man used these things to make the various needed articles, and how the great ships were employed to carry the goods to and fro, and how the different things were exchanged, interested him.

Many of the subjects were not within his comprehension. Why were all these things done? What was the object of having so many products?

John told him that when men had everything they really needed to keep them alive and in comfort, they still wanted something more, and those things were called luxuries; then, after they and their children used these luxuries for a while, they found them to be absolutely essential and they then became necessaries. In that way men learned the use of so many, many things, that the whole world was being searched to find products which would serve to make the needed things.

"Do you mean," said the Chief, "that your people are trying to find things they do not need, so they can buy them, and try to make some use of them?"

John could not help but smile at the acuteness of the question. "That, in effect, is just what they do. It is not so considered, however, by our people. It is difficult to say just where necessity ends and luxury begins. But each year, yes every month, new things are brought out, and people begin to buy them, because the traders and the people who sell are shrewd and know how to cultivate taste and the desire for new and startling things."

"But how do the people get the articles to exchange for these things?"

"The people do not accumulate articles to buy other articles with. Instead, they work to get money, and with this money they buy the things."

"I do not know what you mean by that. What is 'money'?"

"It is an article which tells what everything else is worth."

"Then it must be wonderful. I would like to see that remarkable thing which can tell what everything else is worth."

John took some of the coins from his pocket. "Here is some of it, which we use on Wonder Island."

The Chief smiled. He held them in his hand. He knew the meaning of the hole in the center. They were intended, as he thought, to be threaded on a string, and used as an ornament.

They fascinated him. He had never seen anything so attractive. He looked at John, while he thought, but did not speak. Then John said: "This is worth one cent, and this larger one five cents."

He compared the two. Finally, he said: "What makes this worth so much more than the other, and why are they worth anything?"

"Because there is so much metal,—so much copper, in each."

"But copper is of no use. I cannot eat it, and it will not clothe me."

"No, but if you have this money then you can get the clothes, and the size of them will tell just how much clothing you can get."

"I do not understand it. Where can I go and get clothing with these round pieces!"

"You must go where the clothing is, or the goods must be brought to you."

"Well, if we are here, at a place where there should be no clothing, or no food, this *money*, as you call it, would not enable me to clothe or feed myself?"

"Assuredly not."

"Then it has no value?"

"No; it merely measures the value of something which I can eat or wear, or use."

"Then why not use a taro root, or a fowl, or wisps of fibre?"

"That would be all right, if we could have a common understanding between us of how much a taro bulb was worth by the side of a bundle of fibre, and how large the bundle should be to exchange fairly with an armful of Amarylla tubers."

On the third day the boys, together with John, a party of the boys, and three natives under the lead of Calmo, started for the northern end of the island. John had now learned that the island was entirely unlike the Wonder Island formation.

The latter was fairly circular in form, whereas the one they were now about to explore was narrow and long. That part of the southern portion which they had carefully examined, in order to learn its agricultural possibilities, was rolling, and in many places had level plateaus, not anywhere at a greater altitude than three or four hundred feet above sea level.

There was higher ground to the north, where the climate was uninviting, so Beralsee said, and it was for that reason they made it a convict colony.

John was anxious to see the people who were exiled from their homes on account of their crimes. Furthermore, he was impressed with the idea that the upper end showed volcanic upheavals, which would be likely to expose mineral formations.

Gruesome tales were current of the ferocity of the convicts. It was no wonder that the poor victims, whom George had prevented from being expelled several days before, regarded their deliverance as such a great blessing.

No one, once condemned, was ever permitted to come back. The condemnation was for all time. Furthermore, it was part of the Chief's unwritten code, that no one who transgressed the law could ever make atonement, or recover his rights.

To be able to meet people so condemned, and to talk with them and get their views, was worth an exertion, surely, and Harry and George were just as enthusiastic at the prospects of the journey.

"That may be some recompense for not finding any caves," said George.

Harry laughed, as he looked at George. "To hear you talk people might think you had caves on the brain."

"Well the caves are the only thing that we have had in the way of sport. And then the treasures!"

"I know that; but I shall not be disappointed if there isn't a cave within five hundred miles."

"Nor I; but John is very anxious, for some reason, to find some particular cave. I'll bet anything that skull we found on the southeast peak of Wonder Island has something to do with it, judging by the way he is caring for the skull, and spending hours in examining it."

"I had forgotten about that," responded Harry. "That brings back my interest, now. But John does not think there are any caves on this island, but he believes that there is another island farther south."

"Is that so!"

"I am sure of it."

"How sure?"

"Well, the chart which John made has this island on it, and a mark which shows something like it directly to the south. I saw that several days ago."

"When did he make the drawing?"

"Since he has been on this island."

Harry emitted a low whistle. "I thought John had something in his mind all along. What do you suppose he expects to find in that particular cave?"

"Well, not money; that's sure. It might be a good idea to do some thinking and searching on our own account."

"I have often wondered, since we have been on Wonder Island, and more particularly, since we landed here, whether it would not be possible to trace some of the unsolved mysteries of Wonder Island to this, or some other island."

"Yes, I have often thought of that. We have gone over every part of that island, and found no trace of the other boat load, that is of the boys who came ashore on the *Investigator's* No. 3. None of the tribes ever knew or heard of that boat, nor was there ever a trace of the members of that crew.

"That is the mystery. Some one brought the boat to the island. Some one took it inland. Some one, a man by the name of Walter, wrote a note addressed to Wright, who was one of the companions of John when he was shipwrecked, but Wright knew nothing of Walter. If the solution of this matter does not lie in some other island, we might as well give it up."

Before describing the events of the journey it is necessary to make a digression, so that we may be able to recount some things which had a bearing on the adventures and experiences of the two boys after they returned.

The natives on Wonder Island, as well as on the island where they now were, wore the most primitive kinds of clothing. The men had the simplest clothing, merely a breech clout, worn about the loins, and the Chiefs usually wore some distinguishing clothing about their shoulders, and usually on their arms.

The women, however, had short skirts, and like their white sisters, abounded in ornaments. Some of them had jackets, to which the trinkets were attached. All delighted in bracelets. These were usually formed like bands around their arms and limbs, and the wealth and importance of the dame was judged from the number so employed.

As a result, when they became great and wealthy, more and more clothing had to be used, to enable them to attach the ornaments. It might be said, that clothing was worn, not for the purpose of covering the body, or for comfort, but in order to serve as a vehicle to attach the much desired trinkets, and the dangling character of these articles seemed to be the great attraction.

For this reason bright and sparkling bits of jewelry were the most sought. It mattered not what they were made of, but the glistening surface had its value to them. Singularly enough, the women on the new island strove to decorate themselves in like manner, and presumably, for the same purpose.

When the savages in Wonder Island were brought out of their crude state, the Professor and George knew that they could not change that fundamental law of nature, nor did they attempt to work a revolution in the minds and characters of the people in this respect.

Within certain limitations such a desire to ornament and render themselves attractive is most laudable. They knew that among the few peoples in the world, where that quality is entirely lacking, they are of the lowest type, and possessed of the least intellect, and that all such are the hardest to cultivate.

Here, as on Wonder Island, the natives understood weaving, the fabrics being of the coarsest character, both in the matter of quality and appearance. The work was necessarily slow and tedious, and the principal work of the women was to weave these articles of wear with the simple tools they had.

When the boys built the looms, and the natives saw the wonderful goods produced, and the dyes prepared to give the fabrics the different hues, the women became most expert weavers, and the natural result was that they vied with each other to make the best articles, and to form them into the most fashionable garments.

When the *Pioneer*, and later their new steamer, *Wonder*, which was now regularly running to one of the great seaports, began to bring in such products as they could not make in the islands, a new impetus was given to the dress designed for women.

Before the boys left for Wonder Island, that place attracted immigrants from the north; they brought their families, and began to engage in the business of exporting the fruits and the fibres, as well as the ores and the dyes from the island. From the white women the native women learned the new art of dressing, and of adornment.

Their coming was not needed to give them the desire, but they were not slow to recognize that their fair-skinned sisters could teach them the refining process.

Muro's wife was the sister of Uraso, the latter a man of naturally strong intellect, and his sister was not behind him in her particular domain. She was at all times the leading spirit in the development of her people, and to her the Professor imparted many of the great secrets, that might be of service.

Stut, the brother of Muro, was second in command of the vessel, and before they left on the mission into the interior, John called in Stut, and in presence of the boys imparted a scheme that met with hearty approval.

It was now an open secret that Sutoto and Cinda were in love. If the Chief knew of it he did not exhibit any alarm, or offer any objections. John knew that courtships on the islands were not usually of long duration. He thought it would be a fine thing to make the wedding a "state affair."

"Now, Stut, I want to entrust you with a mission to the

Professor and Muro's wife, to whom you can explain the situation. She must prepare a suitable outfit for the bride, and tell her I think she and the other women that she might choose should also come over. They must not forget to bring the proper costumes for Cinda's mother and for all the attendants.

"The Professor will know what is suitable to send over for the Chief. All this will take some time to arrange, and it must be done without letting Sutoto know. I will arrange the matter with him so that he will not suspect your real mission.

"Our work at the northern part of the island will take about ten days, and probably less. If you have no trouble, and this time of the year is not a stormy one, you can easily make the trip there in a day and a half, and return in the same time, thus giving you a full week to prepare the articles."

Stut was in raptures at the announcement. John knew that he was capable, and trusted him. Shortly afterwards Sutoto was sent for, and John said: "It is necessary for the *Pioneer* to return to Wonder Island to get some things of importance for us. It would please me better to have you remain, and Stut can take your place for the trip; but if you prefer to go, it will be satisfactory."

Sutoto hesitated for a moment. He eyed John for a moment, and the boys begged him to remain. They knew, as did John, that their entreaties were not necessary. Finally, with a most suspicious glance, he consented to stay. Stut was notified, and he came in.

"Stut, I have some very valuable papers which must be delivered to the Professor, who will send some things back, and I have arranged with Sutoto that he shall remain and help us in our investigations here, while you sail the *Pioneer* to Unity."

Stut looked at Sutoto for a moment, as though taken by surprise, and announced his willingness to go. "Then start at once," remarked John, "and return as soon as possible."

Sutoto called Stut aside, after they left John. "Will you get some things for me?" he asked.

"Certainly, what can I do for you?"

Then Sutoto imparted the secret of his coming marriage to Stut, and the latter with well concealed surprise, promised secrecy, and assured him that he would get the clothing necessary and the particular presents that seemed to be of more importance to him than his garments.

Within two hours the ship was ready, and as they were leaving the vessel Stut told the boys of the commission which he had undertaken at Sutoto's request.

CHAPTER XII

THE SKELETON BENEATH THE BOAT

The present journey reminded the boys of the time when they began their wanderings in the unknown wilds of their own island. Then they were inexperienced, lacking the most ordinary knowledge of life in the open, afraid of slightest noise when in unknown places, and constantly fearing attack by wild men or beasts.

What a difference now! They had been successful, and had abundant treasures at their command. Something told them that they were to find still greater treasures, and the zest was one beyond expression.

The course was directed due north. The boys knew that they were to investigate the mountains, the hills and the streams. They were to learn what fruits and vegetation might be found in their native state on the island; the kinds and varieties of animals, and the qualities of the minerals, if the geological formations offered them for inspection.

From the first day that they landed, the boys had heard a peculiar guttural sound, impossible to describe. The sound was almost annoying after they had heard it for a time. Passing the limb of a tree during the first hour of the march they heard the same cry.

"I see what it is," remarked George. "It is a bird. See it on that limb?"

John looked, and then turned to George. "Why certainly, that is the Kagu."

"Why its bill and feet are red, while the rest of the body is gray. What a funny feather it has running back from its head!"

Harry laughed, as he remarked: "I wonder if our women took their hat fashions from the Kagu?"

"You have made a correct observation. Some species of the hornbill have feathers which project up into the air like sentinels, and the same feathers are used in exactly the same fashion by makers of millinery. Now, I am not an authority on the fashions, but I have often thought that if the leaders in styles would build those wonderful head decorations something like the patterns furnished by nature they would be more beautiful and becoming."

"I wonder if it has only one leg?"

John laughed. "I imagine it has two. It is the custom of many birds of this species to stand for hours on one leg. It is of the same family as the stork, the heron and the ibis."

"Why don't we see more animals?"

"The island is not, probably, large enough. These small islands have only the smallest kinds. Besides, the larger animals are found where the nature of the country permits them to conceal themselves."

George stopped before a large bush which had rows of yellow flowers growing up all along the stems, and at each flower was a seed.

"Ah! you have found a most valuable plant," said John, as he broke off one of the stems. "Feel the crushed leaves."

"It is just like grease."

"It is an oil. It is one of the products largely used in the United States, as a substitute for olive oil, and for soap making."

"What is it called?"

"The plant is known as Benne. The product is Sesame oil. The peculiarity of the plant is that nearly one-half of the leaf is a pure oil, and it can remain exposed a long time before it turns rancid."

"I wonder if that is what they use in their cooking!"

"Yes; it is absolutely inodorous, and is better than lard for table uses. Look at the seeds. They are classed with the most nutritious in the world."

"The Chief had them, and I tried some of them the first night I dined with him."

The route led to an upper plateau, well wooded, many of the trees being of the palm variety, with plenty of silver-leafed families so common everywhere.

"Do look at the Coffee trees?" exclaimed Harry.

The Chief's son was consulted. He had no knowledge of the

use of the berry. "We must take a lot of the berries back with us. This will be a treat at the celebration." John stopped short, and the boys commenced to laugh. He had almost given away the scheme for the wedding feast. Sutoto did not catch the force of the allusion.

George and Harry were now on the quest for new things in every direction, and the natives aided them in carrying out their every wish. After they had reached a small stream flowing to the north it became evident that they had passed the highest point of the plateau, and were now descending.

One of the natives pointed out a peculiarly-shaped tree, tall, with immense leaves, and at each leaf cluster there was an immense white flower.

"Here is a tree with yellow flowers. We must have some of these as specimens," said Harry.

The trees were exceedingly tall. "The men are asking if you want some of the flowers," said Sutoto.

"By all means," answered George. Without a moment's hesitation a young athlete made his way to the top, and gathered a dozen branches, which he dropped to the ground.

The beauty of these flowers is difficult to describe. The tree body is perfectly straight, and the limbs grow out uniformly on three sides, the leaves being very rough.

"This is a species which belongs to the Indicus family," remarked John, as he cut off one of the leaves. "It would be a good tree for carpenters to raise."

"Why so?" asked George.

"You see it is just like sand-paper."

"Well, that is something to know. But will it really smooth down wood?"

"It is frequently used for that purpose, and you might take some along and try it."

At intervals John was observed taking up bits of soil, which he carefully wrapped up and deposited in one of the receptacles.

"I am curious to know what you are taking dirt for?" said Harry.

"I should have told you that a knowledge of the nature of the soil is one of the things that is very important to the agriculturist. Many men have made failures because they planted things which the earth was not adapted to grow."

"It has always been a wonder to me why things really do grow up out of the dirt," said Harry.

"That is not difficult to understand, if you will consider that the ground contains food, and that a plant can grow only where it can get the right kind. Then, there may be plenty of food but not the kind it can digest."

"Well, that is news to me. Do plants digest food?"

"Yes, just the same as what we call living animals. The tree is somewhat different from animals, in the particular that it digests its food first and then consumes it afterwards. In this particular certain larvae act the same as trees, that is digest it before they consume it."

"What do you mean by larva?"

"The early form of certain living organisms, before they are fully developed. Thus, the tadpole is the larva of the frog. A great many insects are bred from what are called grubs, or caterpillars. All these are called larva."

"What kind of food is found in the earth?"

"Many, many kinds. Carbon, nitrogen, the various salts, such as lime, magnesia, strontia, and the like, and when the little feelers shoot out from the roots, they are in search of something to eat."

At this point they were interrupted by shouting and laughter from one section of the searching party, and the boys ran out across the open to learn its cause. Two of the natives were carrying a dark brown object, about half the size of an ordinary hog.

It was kicking vigorously, but did not appear to be at all vicious.

"Why, it looks just like a little bear," said George as he danced about. "Let us keep it for a pet."

"It is a bear," said John. "It is the Bruang, or the sun-bear of the Malayan peninsula."

"But doesn't it grow any bigger?"

"No; that is a full size specimen; in fact, it is a pretty large specimen, I should judge."

"What beautiful fur, and so soft! Will it bite?"

"I am of the opinion they can bite, but they are easily tamed and make great pets. Hasn't it a fine white spot on its breast?"

The men stood about and allowed it to move about within the circle. It cast its eyes around, as much as to say: "Well, what are you going to do about it?"

George cried out: "Hold it for a minute," and he pounced on one of the provision bags, and brought out a pot of honey. He forced his way in among the watchers, and with a stick dipped into the honey held it up before the animal.

It smelled the honey, and began to lick the stick, and then it darted for the pot. "What a tongue," exclaimed Harry.

"That is what they are noted for. The tongue is made for the very purpose of going into deep holes, and the greatest use is to rob the hives of the wild honey bee."

The antics of George and the bear were most amusing to the watchers, and occasioned roars of laughter. When the pot was emptied he wanted more, and nosed around George until the latter could hardly keep his feet.

"He is getting to be a mighty close friend," said John, when he could find time to stop laughing for a moment.

"Well, don't let him get away," cried George, as he saw the cordon around the animal broken up, leaving plenty of opening for it to get away.

But, of course, the natives didn't understand him, and soon Mr. Bear had all the opportunity in the world to go home. But he didn't. He walked alongside of George, and the latter liked to stroke his soft fur, to which no objection was offered.

The bear followed and was by his side every minute of the time for the next hour, and while they sat down to lunch little Sunny, as George named him, was at the feast. He had samples of everything in sight, and the menu tasted good, from honey at the beginning of the repast, to honey at the end of it.

* * * * *

The progress was necessarily slow, because there were so many things to examine and to make notes of. They went out of the way from the direct route, so as to cover as wide an area as possible. Before camping for the night they had ascended a slight elevation, and there, to the right and to the left they saw the wide stretches of the great ocean.

Directly ahead was a narrow tongue of land, leading to a broadening area, and off in the dim distance was a high point. The Chief's son pointed there and said:

"On the other side of that high place is where the bad people live."

"That must be a long way off," said John. When this was interpreted he answered: "Another day's march."

The gentle breeze from the eastern shore was a great relief.

They had marched during the day mostly through forests, and everywhere the atmosphere was close and still, so that the open space was appreciated.

All slept soundly that night, and morning came only too soon for the wearied boys, but they enjoyed the trip too much to delay moving at the earliest opportunity. While breakfast was being prepared the boys sauntered over to the sloping shore to the west, which was not more than a half mile away.

They enjoyed walking along the pure white sand, and after disrobing had a jolly time in the mildly moving surf. It was not often that they had opportunities to take a sea bath.

The bathing place was a deeply-indented bay, with a long sloping beach,—an ideal spot, with the camp plainly visible to the east. "Why not take a stroll to the southern end of the bay?" remarked Harry, after they were ready to return. "We might be able to see the headland to the south where we first sighted land."

"Well, then, here goes it," and George started on a strong sprint to the south.

Harry was by far the fleeter, and reached the tufted grass ahead of George, and then turned to the right, to gain the elevation. It was while thus moving through the brush and debris, which was far above the normal level of the sea, that they were attracted by an unusual deposit of brush, and other accumulations.

"Stop, Harry; here is something we ought to investigate."

Harry turned and came back. In the early days of their investigation such a mass would have meant diligent search. It was more from a recurrence of the old habit that dictated the idea to George.

It was well they did so, for not far from the top, and covered over with seaweed and leaves, was a boxlike structure, evidently some part of a wreckage. They worked feverishly at the surrounding mass, and uncovered it.

Harry started back. "Do you know what this is?" he asked.

George stooped over, and stared.

"It is part of the boat which was taken from South River."

When that boat disappeared, only to be found miles away from its original location, the two boxlike compartments which they had made in it, and the oars used by them, had been taken away, and instead they found entirely different oars, and a rope, of which they knew nothing.

Here was one of the boxes. "Let's open it," said George in the most intense tone. That was easily done, and there they found, to their surprise, one of their original shell hatchets, part of a coarsely-woven cloth, which they recognized as one of their early productions on the first loom, and a dozen or more gourds, in which food had been placed, and all exactly as it had been stored away by them. The food had disappeared, of course, but it had been lost by the action of the sea, and decomposition, as it was evident that the contents had not been disturbed by any one.

"Let us call John," said Harry, and he bounded up the beach, and ran over the crest, waving his arms as he did so. He had not gone half the distance before those at the camp saw Harry running, and John, and most of those in sight started on a run, George meanwhile industriously dragging away the debris.

"We have found it," cried Harry, as John came within hailing distance, and without waiting for them to come up he bolted back.

"Now what have you discovered?" asked John as he came up breathless.

"Part of our old boat."

"We thought George had met with some accident."

"We got this by accident," answered George. "See, here are some more things. This is the oar we had. How can you explain that?"

It was certainly a poser. Why the exchange of oars? John shook his head. For once he had no theory even to offer. "Come, boys, let us take away all this stuff."

All gave a hand, Sutoto wondering why there should be so much ado about a bit of wreckage. George explained the affair, as well as he could.

"What is that board?" exclaimed John. "No, not a board; that is part of a boat," he added as more of the accumulation was torn away.

"It's a boat; it's a boat!" almost shrieked George.

"Come to this end and take away this lot of seaweed," called out Harry.

They soon uncovered a boat with one end embedded in the sand so it was difficult to turn it over, owing to the rotten condition of the wood. Only here and there was any paint visible. The action of the elements had done its work.

"What kind of a boat was this?" asked Harry.

John did not answer, but peered down on the sand where the prow had rested. "Take away the sand carefully here," he said, and when he pointed the boys saw something white protruding an inch or two.

As the sand was scraped away they first saw the thigh bone

of a skeleton, and soon the whole frame was laid bare, the interstices filled with sand. A peculiar rope was around the frame, and John grasped it.

The boys eagerly looked at it as John intently examined it. "It is the same," he said.

"The same as what?" asked Harry.

"The same as the rope found on the boat when you discovered it on the beach."

That was the first time that the boys knew that John had any idea about the loss of the boat, or of the strange rope. It was possible, however, that the Professor had told John about it, as they were accustomed to talk over these strange things.

"But the boat?" asked George. "What do you think of the boat?"

"It is the exact counterpart of the *Investigator's* Life boat No. 3."

CHAPTER XIII

A CONVICT COLONY OF NATIVES

The Chief's son was present. "Did you ever know of a boat load of castaways on the island?" asked John.

"We never knew of anything like that," was his reply.

Every scrap in that mass of wreckage was gone over. There was nothing else visible by which they could gain the slightest clue. The skeleton was minutely examined. It was that of a strong, well-developed man, but from all appearances one leg was shorter than the other.

The bones of the shortened leg were closely investigated. "The bones show that this man met with an accident in early life, or before he was fully grown, or, he may have had some disease before he attained full growth, so that his right leg is shorter because not fully developed," said John, as he continued the examination.

"He must have been a soldier or an adventurer, as he has three bullet marks, one here in the right shoulder, one in the ankle, and the other on the cheek bone. All of the wounds were healed before he met his death."

"But there is one thing which is still more remarkable. This man was a captive. He was tied in the boat and it was set adrift, and was likely on the open sea and washed ashore during one of the monsoons."

"Why do you think so?" asked Harry, as soon as he could recover breath after this announcement.

"This rope tells the story."

"But how does it happen that he and the boat were together. It seems to me that if the waves were high enough to bring the boat clear up to this point, he would be freed from the boat long before it reached this place."

"He was tied to the boat."

One mystery was solved, and another more terrible in its aspect came upon its heels. There was but one thing to do, and that was to bury the skeleton, and John ordered this done, as soon as he had taken the complete measurements of the remains.

"We don't want the box or the things in it now," said Harry.

"Indeed, I want the hatchet," answered George.

"Yes, and the rope," added John.

The boys went back to the camp with thoughtful expressions on their faces.

"This seems to be a Wonder Island, too," said George, more to himself than to any one else.

They descended the incline, and crossed the narrow neck of

land that joined the two parts of the island. Beyond, as they advanced the ground grew more uneven and rugged. Occasionally rocks appeared, the first that they had noticed except around the place where George was captured.

Nevertheless, vegetation grew in even greater profusion than on the other branch of the island. There were more berries upon which all the natives feasted, and the boys were not slow to pick them as they passed.

In traveling alongside of a hill Harry was the first to call attention to a peculiar leaf on a plant, which bore rose-shaped flowers. "This is something new to me. There is nothing like it on Wonder Island. Did you notice it, John?"

The latter took a branch, and gazed at it for a long time. "I am surprised to find this growing here. It is a plant well known in Palestine, and is called the Rose of Jericho."

"What a delightful perfume it has," said Harry.

"It is not noted on that account, however. It is the *resurrection* plant."

"How singular; and in what way did it get that name?"

"It may be dried up entirely, and if placed in water it will again appear to revive and raise itself up. This is, of course, due to its power to absorb a vast amount of water. It is found near the shores of the Dead Sea, and I recall that when I was in Jerusalem it was a common thing to see the plant in its dried-up state, sold to pilgrims who were instructed how to resurrect it."

Here was caught the second and only other animal on the trip. It was somewhat smaller than Sunny, and the latter danced about the dead animal, as the "boys" brought it in.

"And what is this big-eared fellow?" asked George.

John laughed as he recognized the apt description. "It is a kind of Australian kangaroo. It inhabits trees, but is very clumsy in appearance and in action. It is a kind of sloth, or wombat."

"Isn't that a dandy fur?"

"The fur is not so valuable as its skin. There is nothing to compare with the softness of the hide when tanned. It feels like the finest velvet, and is very strong and durable."

They were now ascending a series of hills, each more difficult than the last, and the ground became extremely rough and broken. There was a lone path, in many places nearly obliterated. It was the uninviting road to the land of sorrow.

The Chief's son tried to be in the company of the boys at all times, and while he could not understand their chatter, Sutoto was a willing interpreter. He enjoyed the jolly freedom of the two chums, and their uniform good nature.

George and Harry were ever on the alert to make him feel at ease and so they talked with him, and told of the things which John explained, and it was plainly seen that he marveled at things which were described.

Referring to the exiled people, George asked: "Do those people never return after they are once condemned?"

"They are never permitted to come back."

"Do they stay there of their own free will?"

"No; I am told that they long to be at home again."

"Well, what would you do if they tried to come back?"

"We would drive them away. One time they tried to come back, all of them, and we had to kill some of them," and he said it in a tone of regret.

"Don't you believe in killing?"

He looked at George for a moment, and then looked up into Sutoto's eyes, as he said: "No; it would do no good. Would that be the right way?" he asked with a sort of innocence that brought a blush to George's cheeks.

"No; we do not believe in killing, except when we must to protect ourselves."

"But do you have to make such wonderful things as those (pointing to the guns) to protect yourselves?"

John threw back his head and tried to prevent a loud laugh, at this perfectly obvious question, while he looked at the boys to see what sort of an answer would be given.

George was non-plussed for a minute. John had no business to disconcert him in that way. He turned and expected Harry to answer, but it seemed as though he had imperfectly understood it. There was no way out of it, and George tried to get his body into a proper position to answer it with dignity.

"Well, you see, the guns were not made for the purpose of killing people, but for sporting purposes."

"Do you have many wild animals in your country?" he asked naively.

"Not many now."

John laughed a little so as not to be too undignified, and George saw the humor of the situation. He did not want to pursue the subject any further, and John graciously turned the conversation by announcing the discovery of the Upas tree.

"I didn't know the Upas tree was of such immense size," said Harry. "Is it really true that it kills everything that comes near it?"

"No, that is greatly exaggerated. The only time when it gives forth any harmful exudations, is when it is cut down, or when the bark is torn away, or it is wounded in such a way that the sap comes into contact with the body."

The illustration shows a flowering branch of the tree, and gives an idea of the silk-like leaves.

They were still going upwardly. On both sides, to the east and to the west could be seen the rolling sea. Ahead was the mountain, if such it might be called. Rocks began to appear everywhere. John stopped long at some of those dark gray walls, and chipped off many specimens.

There were now fewer birds and animals, except very small species, such as squirrels, and a variety of weasel, quick in its movements and reddish in color.

"This begins to look promising," remarked John, as he crawled around the ledges.

"Do you think we shall find any caves here?" asked George.

"I shall be very much surprised if we do not," he answered.

"Isn't it singular that the natives never knew about them, if there are any here?"

"No; I do not think that is strange; they do not believe in the witch doctors, and they have no Krishnos here, so that the caves are of no value to them."

"But do you find much that is valuable in the way of ores?"

"The hills here are full of the most valuable minerals. The little prospecting I have done is sufficient to satisfy me on that point. I am trying to make a fair estimate so I can give an accurate report when we return."

It was late in the afternoon when they reached the summit of the mountain which they had viewed from the south. It was green to the very summit, and from the elevation where they stood they could see a long and narrow stretch to the north, the distance in that direction being much farther than they had traveled from the little bight of land on the south.

"It does look inviting in that part of the island," said Harry. "Were you ever there, in the bad place?" asked Harry as the Chief's son came up.

"No; but I have heard much about it."

One of the natives who heard the conversation said: "It is a beautiful place."

"Have you ever been there?" he was asked.

"I was a guard on two occasions when we took prisoners there," he answered.

"Tell us about it," said George.

"I have never been in the village, but within an hour's march of it. The Chief warned us never to go into the place itself."

Aside from the village the place which interested John and the boys most was the mountain on which they were now standing. This must be explored. It was now late in the afternoon, and at John's suggestion they encamped, and only short excursions were made by the boys in the quest for something new.

It was a delightful night. The elevation gave them the advantage of a beautiful breeze, and the odors wafted to them, from some unknown source, on the mild trade wind from the north, was almost like a narcotic, so soothing and restful.

"Did you ever visit a more delightful spot?" asked Harry, as he inhaled the beautiful perfume.

"It does not seem to me that the criminal colony is in a very bad place, if this is any indication of it. Isn't that way of dealing with crime a strange thing?" remarked George.

"Why so?" asked John. "Is it anything peculiar for the wrongdoers to be banished from a community?"

"No; but it seems wrong to condemn the innocent women and children. Why should they be punished along with the guilty?"

"Probably, in the majority of cases, the women and children

would prefer to accompany their husband and father. That does not seem to be so cruel, when it is considered that they are left free to live as much so as in their own community."

"That is what I cannot understand. What is the use of sending them away, if they are not locked up?"

"Do you not know that among the ancients, banishment from a country was the greatest punishment; greater even than death, in the opinion of many; and there are many cases where suicide was preferable. The odium of banishment was so great in those days that only the strongest and the greatest of men could live it down."

"It makes me feel, when I smell this delightful perfume, that the home of the bad people over there must be a beautiful place," said George.

"To give such an opinion, just because of the fragrance that comes from the north is proper for a sentimentalist," said John, as he laughed.

"Well, that is a pretty big name to give, and I suppose it means having some notion that hasn't any sense in it, but just theory?"

"That is a fairly close description, but I didn't mean it in that way."

The boys never felt resentful at anything that John might say, as they knew and appreciated his noble character and disposition too well not to understand that his remarks were never born of malice.

After a restful night preparations were made for a complete survey of the mountain, if it might be so dignified. Its greatest altitude did not exceed eight or nine hundred feet, and the width of the island at this point did not exceed two miles. It was quite rugged toward the east, but on the western side of the island the descent was sloping, and offered easy examination.

The natives were instructed what to do, and were told that they should particularly hunt for caves, or great holes, or entrances into the hills. Four search parties were thus organized, John being at the head of one, and George, Harry and Sutoto, each being a leader in the others.

Sutoto was most competent for work of this kind, as he had accompanied the boys on many expeditions, and was anxious to be of service in the quest.

John took a direction to the northeast, and Sutoto to the southeast, thus leaving Harry and George with their parties to explore the region to the west, and northwest.

As they were separating George slyly remarked: "John must have had some particular reason for taking the direction he did."

Harry smiled. "I hope we shall find the first caves."

Before separating John told them that he was desirous of finding a cavern which had certain peculiar markings therein, and the description showed it to be Cross-shaped. This must not be forgotten.

They entered into the undertaking with the greatest enthusiasm.

The boys simply danced, as they went down the hill, so great was the joy and the freedom of that beautiful spot. What a wonderful sensation is produced by beautiful odors. It is like a thought which transports you. On the other hand, when the odors are disagreeable how it depresses and disgusts.

A great French physician has said that in his observations, the real happy people are those who delight in beautiful odors; and while it is not true that criminals are devoid of the elevating influence of delightful perfumes, still, they are less influenced thereby.

In a number of tests made some years ago, a curious fact was observed: Sweet odors were allowed to Teach sleeping patients, which, when they did excite dreams, made them feel that they were living in a world of bliss, and surrounded by all the luxuries of life. On the other hand, when exposed to evil smelling odors, they dreamed of miseries, and of trouble and disgrace.

It was understood that the different expeditions were to report at the camp at midday, and that in the event of any accident, or other mishap, the firing of the guns would be sufficient warning to the party at the camp and to those who were searching.

George had with him two of his own "boys," and two of the natives, and Harry was also accompanied by several of his particular favorites. Harry, with his party, was the energetic one, as he was exceedingly wiry and a good walker. He did not intend to permit the others to encroach on any of his territory.

Not a vestige of anything was found which even so much as pointed to a cave or to the sign of human occupancy in that section. George, on the other hand, was more fortunate. In his area the shelving rocks were more numerous, and he also knew that the rocks were limestone, and that caves were more likely to exist in limestone formation than in trap rock, or either in granite or sandstone formations.

He was, therefore, fully prepared, when, in the early part of his investigation, to find, what appeared to be entrances, but in all cases they were blind leads,—that is they led in for short distances only, many of them being mere cleavages of the rocks.

The real cave is the one where the limestone is eaten out by the erosive action of the water attacking the calcium of the rock. Furthermore, he felt that he must go down nearer sea level to be assured of success, and he acted on that impulse.

Roger Thompson Finlay

CHAPTER XIV

A WHITE PARALYTIC IN THE CONVICT COLONY

It would be useless to recount the experiences of all of the parties. They had four hours of search before them. This would, at least, give some idea as to the nature of the mountain, and enable John to decide whether it would be wise to give that project further consideration.

At midday the parties began to appear, first Harry, then Sutoto, followed by John, and finally George. The latter was the only one who was smiling. The three early parties had no news to impart.

"What have you found?" were the hailing words of George, as he approached.

"Nothing! nothing!" were the answers.

"It takes me to bring home the goods," he remarked, and Harry laughed in derision.

"No; but I mean it," he continued. "I have captured a modern, good-sized cave, and it is now awaiting to be explored."

John could not believe the tale. "You are to be congratulated. Good boy!" Needless to add, George was the happiest person in that camp.

"Let us go down to see it at once," said George in his eagerness. "It is quite a distance, as it is not more than five hundred feet from the seashore."

"Luncheon first," remarked John, and no one interposed an objection, as the trip had sharpened the appetites of all.

The meal over little time was lost in making a start, and George led the way with his boys. Truly enough, there was the open mouth, and it was cave-like. Now for the mysteries within. "We went in only about a hundred feet, so as to be sure we weren't fooled," said George, in reference to his discovery.

The lamps were then prepared, and all the preparations made, the boys being veterans in this sort of work, and John was ahead, as was generally the custom in these expeditions.

"This is as far as we went," said George. Beyond was still a wall which glistened from the streaming lights.

Gradually the walls came closer together; the track was a narrow one; so they had to march in single file. John called a halt. "I am afraid this is a blind hole," he said, but George could not believe it, so the side walls were searched, for indications of some opening.

"This is the end of the cave. Note the side walls. If they should be pressed against each other they would fit exactly, showing that it is an opening caused by a fissure and not by erosion."

Harry could not help but laugh. All this time lost on a blind lead, and the laugh was on George.

Harry could not help jesting him. "If you are a good tribe finder it is no sign that caves are in your line."

John enjoyed the laugh on George, but the latter retorted: "I think the joke is on you, for traveling all this distance to see a hole in the ground."

There was not the sign of a cave on the island, aside from the one discovered (?) by George, so the party remained that night at the mountain top, and in the morning descended the hill, and slowly marched to the north. Before noon they entered a beautiful stretch of woodland, with luxurious grass growing all around in profusion.

"This is as far as the guards have been permitted to go," said one of the natives, who had volunteered the information about the place the day before.

Thus far not a human being was visible. An hour's march would bring them to the village of the criminals, and the boys began to examine their weapons, and to look apprehensive.

The wild fruits of the tropics were now seen in abundance in every direction. Bananas, the Bread Fruit, Cocoa, and Date Palm, on every hand.

The most astonishing thing, however, was the profusion of flowers, of every variety, seemingly, and the air was scented as with one vast bouquet.

Sutoto stopped and pointed ahead: "They are in the trees gathering fruit." The party halted, and looked, and then proceeded.

They were, undoubtedly, the first of the criminals. A half mile beyond, and in a plain road, were several of the inhabitants. Those in the trees, two men and a boy, descended, and, together with two women, walked across the field, to witness the newly-arrived criminals, as they supposed.

They were astounded at the appearance of the party. The Chief's son addressed the men, and told them who they were, and their mission. As this was the first time that such a visit had ever been made, the man instructed the boy to run to the village and inform the people, and he scurried away.

Meantime the party moved on, and, as they proceeded, more and more of the inhabitants were seen. To the right were people in the fields, engaged in some sort of work there. This was singular. Nothing of that kind was seen in the village where Beralsee was chief.

"What is the name of this town where the convicts live?" asked Harry.

"Hutoton," replied Calmo.

"And what is the name of your town?"

"Sasite."

"Rather queer names, I should say," exclaimed Harry.

John laughed and glanced at Harry, as he said: "I wonder how *Unity*, and *Pioneer*, and *Mayfield*, and the queer English names sound to them!"

"Oh, I suppose they have some good reason for having such names."

"Yes; for the same reason that we apply names to certain things. See what a wonderful expression there is in the word 'Harsh,' and how expressive it is compared with its opposite 'soft.' How the first word grates, and the second comes out so smoothly. Then, compare 'swift' and 'slow'; or 'sweet' and 'sour.' Ugh! I can almost taste the last word."

John roared, as he saw the serious aspect of Harry's face. But other sights now attracted their attention. A group of men and women appeared. How strange the natives looked. They were well dressed, that is, judged from the people in Sasite, and they were people of good deportment, if those of the inhabitants that accompanied them were fair specimens.

At the head of the villagers was a man of striking appearance, tall, with white hair, such as you would call distinguished, because he differed from most around him. The women were well clad, and the children plump and vigorous in their actions.

Something must be wrong! These people were not criminals! The old man came forward, and gave a respectful bow. He looked at John and said a few words. Calmo responded, his words when translated being: "These are friends of my father, and they have come to visit you."

At this the man gave another bow, and John went up and held out his hand, which the man took in a simple and unaffected manner.

"We welcome you to our village," was his reply.

The boys looked at each other and relaxed their hold on the guns. Was this, after all, the wicked place that had been described to them? As they marched down to the village they were enchanted at the flowers which greeted them on all sides.

Here and there were garden spots, carefully kept, and when the first huts appeared beyond the grove, the boys simply gasped, and could hardly believe their senses. Hundreds of Magnolia trees were in bloom; and the gentle breeze blowing in from the sea, moderated the rays of the sun, and wafted the odor of the plants many miles inland.

The homes were not rudely built, and, although they were on the same general plan of those in Sasite, they had every appearance of comfort.

The head man of the village led them to a more pretentious home, probably his own dwelling. This was soon confirmed, as they were invited to enter and repose themselves on slightly elevated couches, so much like Chief Beralsee's court.

Within a short time there was a great commotion in the village. The boys looked around startled, and the old man noticed it, for he turned to Calmo, and said: "The villagers are preparing a feast for you. Let them go out and mingle with the people."

The boys were happy at this opportunity of satisfying their curiosity. Sutoto accompanied them, and with Calmo, they placed themselves under the guidance of a young man named Anasa, who, Calmo said, was the son of the old man.

They passed down the main street, for there was some semblance of order in the location of the huts. Around the huts were flowers, just as they had seen on the path leading from the mountain, and here and there patches of growing vegetables. After passing one rather attractive looking hut, Anasa paused for a moment, and then turned back, motioning for them to follow. He entered, and the boys saw a villager, and two women within.

Anasa pointed to the figure of a man seated in a chair, and upon seeing it both boys started back in amazement.

"That is a white man," cried Harry.

Anasa nodded, his manner indicating that he felt sure that the boys would recognize him as belonging to their race. George went up to him, and held out his hand. In response the man gave a listless look, and slowly raised the left hand, which was grasped by George, who said: "I am glad to see you. Who are you? We are white, the same as you are."

The man made no sign, and his arm dropped to his side as George relaxed his grasp. Harry touched George on the shoulder, as he said: "There is something the matter with him. Ask Anasa about him."

Calmo put the question, and this was the reply: "We found the poor fellow on the beach many moons ago. We brought him here, and tried to heal him, but he does not speak, and one side of him has no life."

The man made no show of recognition, and the only motion observable was a twitching jerk of the left arm, and a slightly swaying motion of the head.

"John must know about this," said George.

"By all means," was the reply.

Calmo was told about the wonderful man John, and that he should be called at once, so one of the accompanying natives was instructed to bring John, and he speeded away on the errand.

George stood outside of the hut when John came up. "This is a remarkable thing. Did they tell you about it?"

"No."

"There is a white man here."

"Where?" asked John in astonishment.

"In the hut, and he is paralyzed and cannot speak."

John did not wait for more, and as he went the head man followed him in. Then they told him the story, and John stood there and gazed at the man. To the boys who were by John's side he remarked: "I do not know him. I do not think I ever saw him before. How long has he been in this condition?" The old man responded: "Ever since we picked him up on the shore, about *tuta romama* ago."

"And how long ago was that?"

George informed him that Calmo received the information that it was over two years prior to that time, and as John received this information he passed his hand over his head, and, turning to Harry, said: "We shall, probably, get at the bottom of another mystery."

"What is it? Why do you think so?" asked George in astonishment.

"Not now; not now!" answered John, wishing to defer discussion until they were out of the stricken man's hearing.

The latter, however, did not in the least appreciate who were before him. He was not at all perturbed by his visitors, nor when John quietly passed his hand along the poor man's arm and body to satisfy himself of the extent of the paralytic stroke.

He winced but slightly when the examination of the left side was made, otherwise there was no sign of comprehension on his part.

"This is a remarkable thing," said John, as they were returning to the old man's dwelling.

"Why, is it a peculiar case?"

"The ailment itself is not remarkable; but there is something which passes my comprehension."

"What is it!" asked the boys in, unison.

"These people are savages."

"Yes; answered the boys."

"And they are criminals," he said as he stopped and looked at the boys, with an earnestness that surprised them.

It did not take more words to make them understand what John meant. These people had taken this shipwrecked man, and tenderly cared for him during a period of more than two years. This was done without hope of reward. John learned later on that the natives of the town had made provision for the shipwrecked man and had compensated the people at whose home he was then living.

After the evening meal, John walked around the village, observing the people, and he found happiness everywhere. Everything seemed to be arranged according to a system. The old man was not a chief, but was looked upon as their advisor and guide; but he was a criminal, as were all the others in that town.

That evening when all were present John had the first opportunity to talk with the venerable chief of the town.

"How long have you been here?" he was asked.

He was silent for a moment and then answered: "Thirty years."

It must be understood that the questions and answers had to be translated and as the natives knew nothing about the division of time in months or years it was necessary to convert the time which was given by nature into terms of years and months.

Thus, they understood what a day meant, and they could calculate time, as all savages do, by the phases of the moon, and in many cases they were able to indicate time by the position of the sun, in which they recognized three phases only, namely, when the sun was directly above them, and when it reached the extreme northern and southern points.

"Why were you sent here?"

"Because I committed a crime."

John was almost startled at the frankness of the confession, which the old man made without the least perceptible show of feeling or shame.

"Would you like to go back again?"

"Go back where?"

"To your home."

He looked bewildered for a moment, and then answered: "This is my home."

"But I mean your old home at Sasite."

The old man shook his head vigorously, and answered: "No! no! There is no place like Hutoton."

"Do you know what 'Hutoton' means?"

"Yes; it means 'the place of death.'"

The boys were startled at the reply. John turned to them, when he saw their expression, and smiled. The old man, too, smiled.

"Do any of your people want to go back?"

He looked surprised at the question. "Do they want to go back?" he repeated the query. "No; but you should ask them. I do not know of any one who wishes to return. We love our Chief too much to wish for such a thing."

"Do you know what the people in Sasite think of this place?"

"No; not altogether; I am curious to know."

"They believe it is a terrible place, and that the people who are sent here never have another day of peace or happiness."

"And have they not changed their opinions? I used to think so too, and we believed it of those who went before us; but we thought they might have changed their opinions, because we felt that people were growing better and not worse. It is a long time since they sent us real criminals, and we thought the Chief's people were growing wiser and happier."

"When did the last criminals come here?"

"Nearly one year ago."

CHAPTER XV

SAVAGE MARRIAGE CUSTOMS

It was impossible to describe the effect of these revelations on the boys. It was so different from anything they had been led to expect. It brought one thing forcibly to their minds; that because these people had committed some crime, or some wrong against society, they were still human beings, and were worthy of being treated as men and women.

John related to them that various governments had tried the plan of sending convicts to some foreign lands, and placing them in situations where they might work out their own salvation; that all such efforts were successful, where real opportunities were bestowed.

"The idea is," remarked John, "that they are banished from the society in which they resided, or in which they were raised, for the purpose of helping them. The reason for inflicting punishment on criminals has been to protect society but apparently no efforts have been made to cure the criminals or to help them to better themselves."

"I heard the Professor say, at one of the trials at Wonder Island, that some scientists consider crime a disease," said George.

"Exactly; now suppose we treated people suffering from smallpox, or scarlet fever, or some other like disease, just like we treat criminals, it would be regarded as brutal. To lock them up, and deprive them of the pleasures of living, simply to protect society, is wrong."

"But the smallpox and scarlet fever patients are taken away so they will not give the complaints to others," observed Harry.

"And that is right. I favor that and advocate that same thing with criminals. But the patients are not deprived of the things they have been accustomed to, and they are restored, when cured. It is not so with the poor unfortunate who errs. When he does come back he is hounded and looked upon as a tainted individual, although he may, in heart, be better than his accusers."

During that day and the next, the natives and those who accompanied John associated with each other, and had many conversations. What interested them was the presence of the unfortunate paralytic who was unable to speak for himself.

The boys did not believe that he was one of the crew of the school ship *Investigator*. What connection, if any, did he have with the skeleton they found the day before? was another of their queries.

On the second day they were taken to the beach where the white man was found. There, as explained, he was found, with wreckage all about, during one of the raging monsoons with which the boys were so well acquainted, but aside from that there was not a vestige to show his name or where he was from.

All the clothing worn by him originally, and of that there

was scarcely any when found, had been worn threadbare, and he was now dressed in native garments. The chair in which he was reclining was undoubtedly from some wrecked ship, and had been in the possession of the villagers for years.

John spoke to the old man concerning the patient, and advised him that they would soon call to take him away. They would thus relieve them of the burden, and endeavor to restore him to health, if it were possible to do so.

The old man was thankful for the kind words uttered by John, and the latter assured him that before many moons passed he would return and show his appreciation for their kindness to a fellow creature.

"But we do not feel that we have done anything which especially merits praise. He is one like ourselves, who was in distress, and we helped him."

"Yes; you have done that which is right. We intend to reward you not that you should be paid for doing what is right, but to show that we appreciate your noble actions," answered John.

The party, after many wishes and hearty good-byes, filed out of the village, some of them loath to go.

Calmo was silent. He was not the same as before they marched through the village. John noticed it, but he wisely refrained from commenting on the sights they had witnessed. There was cleanliness and order in Hutoton; and filth and disorder in Sasite. It was impossible to be unconscious of the difference between the industry in one place, and the utter shiftlessness in the other.

As it required two days to make the return journey, they

were absent from Sasite nearly seven days, and, according to the calculations, the *Pioneer* would be in from Unity within the next two days.

During the intervening time the boys roamed at will through the island, and on the second day went directly south, so as to scour the sea front below the village.

In the afternoon, as they were about to return, they saw a sail, George being the first to catch a glimpse of it. "The *Pioneer*," he cried, upon which they danced about in sheer joy and started for the village, which was distant several miles.

They were almost out of breath when they rushed through the village, and cried out the news. Everybody was expectant; all were eager to see the vessel come in and Sutoto was the first to reach the landing.

During the visit of the boys on the island, John had a crude dock constructed, and as the *Pioneer* was of light draft, this was not a difficult thing to do, so that the passengers could land from the ship directly on the solid platform.

The Chief was among the merry villagers. "Who is that man with the white hair!" he asked of Uraso.

The latter was just as much surprised as his questioner, when he recognized the Professor, and he informed the Chief of the treat he would experience in meeting him. "He is the Great Wise man," added Uraso, "whom everybody loves."

Muro, too, was astounded as the Professor came down. But a still greater surprise awaited the two chiefs. Muro's wife hailed him, and then Uraso's wife waved her handkerchief. This was too much for them, and waving aside all dignity they rushed forward to greet them.

The whole thing had been so admirably arranged, that no one knew of the affair which had been planned by John. Sutoto joined in the merriment, but he was too anxious to see Stut to pay much attention to the greetings.

The visitors discreetly refrained from saying a word to Sutoto, concerning the coming event. Besides the Chief's wives, there were several other women, of the Tribes in Wonder Island, together with some white men and their wives, who had been invited at the request of Blakely.

The latter greeted John with that hearty expression so characteristic of the true commercial man, and he was not with John a minute before he was plying all sorts of questions about the resources of the island, the kind and number of inhabitants the nature of the soil, and the possibilities of mineral development.

The Professor came down and was introduced to the Chief by Uraso.

The great burly chief was fascinated. He gazed on the Professor and almost gasped, then turning to Uraso he said: "Ah! I know why he is a wise man."

To Uraso this remark was indeed a puzzle; to think that the Chief had discovered the secret of the wisdom in the Professor! He was quick to ask why he knew it.

"Because he has double eyes."

Uraso laughed, and turned to the Professor, to whom he related the incident. Instantly the Professor removed the glasses, and courteously handed them to the Chief, and

Uraso adjusted them to the Chief's eyes.

He glanced around, through the lens, and forced out one expression of delight after the other. He was oblivious of everything else. He forgot that there were dozens of the visitors ready in line to be introduced to him; but all enjoyed the great pleasure he experienced in the new sight.

But suddenly he stopped in his enthusiasm, and with an apology took off the glasses and held them up, in the act of handing them back. The Professor returned them, and took another pair from his pocket which he put on.

It was not likely that the Chief could have received a more acceptable present, as his eyesight was failing, and the glasses seemed like the opening of a new world to him. Later on the Professor provided a pair of glasses better adapted to his sight.

The Chief then became concerned about the comfort of his guests, so Uraso said: "Do not feel worried about the visitors. They will sleep on the vessel where they have comfortable rooms."

The Chief could hardly believe the statements, as he muttered: "This is, indeed, wonderful."

It would require pages to record the incidents that came to his attention about the wonders of these new people. The surprising thing was, that Uraso, and the natives of Wonder Island were dressed like the white people and acted like them, and yet he was told that all that wonderful change had come about in a little over two years' time.

Muro's wife was quickly made acquainted with the Chief's wife, and the day following she had a consultation with her.

Mida, who was Muro's wife, said: "I do not know whether or not you know of Sutoto's affection for Cinda, but we learned about it, and have come over to attend the ceremony."

Linnea, the Chief's wife, smiled as Mida spoke to her. "Yes, I know of it, but the Chief has not yet been told."

It seems that they had very curious and at the same time different customs among the various tribes, and Mida's object was to learn what their etiquette called for as to betrothals. Among some of the Wonder Island tribes, the Chief was the only one who has the right to consent to the marriage of the females, although the males could go to other tribes and secure wives without the consent of the Chief.

In other tribes the women, the mothers, are the sole judges, and it is not infrequent for the parents of the bride to demand a payment, dependent on the rank or the riches of the father.

Then the question of ceremonies is always an important one. It would be sacrilegious to perform the rite except in exact accordance with the prescribed rules. Sometimes those rules are so extremely different to those of another tribe that intermarriage between members of such tribes is impossible.

Thus, a Tuolo could never marry a Saboro, nor could an Illya warrior take an Osaga for a bride. On all these points the women were adepts. It is more than likely, however, that Cinda and Sutoto had all that matter fully understood between them.

"Did Stut tell you about Sutoto?" asked George.

Harry laughed. "No; but I have a good one to tell you. What did he say?"

"Well, you know he hired Stut to get him a wedding outfit, and a present?"

"Yes."

"When the people left the vessel Sutoto sneaked back, and hunted up Stut. Of course Stut had the package all done up, and he is now taking it over to his hut."

"I have something better than that. Sutoto is going to be married to-night."

"How do you know?"

"Cinda told one of her girl friends, and it frightened her so that she told Uraso."

"Why that would spoil all the plans."

"So it would, but Uraso told his sister."

"Are you sure of that?"

"Of course I am; I was there."

"What did she say?"

"She simply said 'I will take care of that.'"

"Of course she will; she's a brick."

CHAPTER XVI

SUTOTO AND CINDA'S MARRIAGE; AND THE SURPRISE

Mida had learned the situation. Their customs as to marriages closely resembled that of the Saboros. In that tribe the Chief was the sole authority. To marry without his consent meant exile for the disobedient warrior, and for the bride as well.

Sutoto was a member of the Berees, and there the mother was the matchmaker. She prescribed all the requirements. The first thing that Mida did was to insist that the Chief should be informed of the desires of the young people.

To the delight of the two women he consented to the match, and he was then told that the people had come over from Wonder Island to take part in the ceremony. But when he was told that they intended to marry that night, by stealth, his brow was clouded.

His law was that no one should marry without his consent, and he could not believe that Cinda could thus attempt to take the matter into her own hand. It was hard to think that his own child should be the first to break his law.

The women pleaded with him, and then Mida confided her plan to him. The tribe's marriage ceremony was a very curious one. First, there must be a gift of fruit, then of fowl, and next of game. This must be brought to the door of the bride by the groom blindfolded.

He must remain blindfolded while she prepares them for the table. Not a word must be spoken, or they must separate forever. A part of the ceremony requires that the invited guests are to resort to every sort of device to make them speak. The slightest sound by either is a sign that they will quarrel, and means the end of the affair.

If they pass this test, the second comes when the bridegroom's eyes are uncovered. They are then to converse with each other, and they must not for a moment relax the talk. Neither has any knowledge of the time that this test must continue. There must be no faltering, or hesitancy.

Mida conferred with John and the boys, as she told of these necessary requirements, and the boys laughed as they listened.

"What is the object of all that?" inquired George.

John was chuckling at the idea, but it stirred up a reminiscence. "That is a custom, in some of its features, that I learned about some tribes in central Africa. I can see the object of that rite. The taking of the gifts blindfolded signifies that he enters the marriage state blindly, and that he must do so in silence, and without asking any questions."

"Of course, then, there is not any likelihood of them quarreling," said Harry.

"That is what the Chief's wife said," replied Mida.

"But what does all the talking mean?"

"That is perfectly obvious. To show they can perfectly agree, even though they do talk."

"But that is all before the real ceremony itself," said George. "How do they get married? That is the main thing."

"Why," said Mida, "that is part of the marrying."

"But they haven't promised anything. Marrying is promising."

This occasioned another roar of merriment. "Yes; marriage is a contract under our law, but not so with these people. The only question with them is whether they are suited to each other."

"But suppose they should not want to marry each other, or one of them should object," interposed Harry.

"Ah! don't you see there is where the prospective bride or groom, in that case has a chance. If, in the first test he should speak, or in the last trial she should fail to keep up the conversation, then it would be all off."

Mida confided her plans to the Chief and his wife. They were assured that Cinda would not think of overriding the well-known laws as to the gifts, and the two tests, and so it was arranged that Sutoto should be permitted to bring his offerings, which he would no doubt do, by stealth, while the Chief and all the visitors were to partake of the banquet on board of the vessel that evening.

Sutoto and Cinda knew of the arrangements for the banquet, and that appeared to be a suitable occasion for them. When Sutoto appeared with the gifts he and Cinda were to be arrested by the Chief's warriors and brought aboard the vessel, charged with violating the law of the Chief in not first obtaining his permission.

The boys remained ashore, and carefully watched the proceedings. How Sutoto got the presents the boys did not know, but they had a suspicion that Cinda had a hand in it. The boys laughed as they saw what a ridiculously short distance he had to go in a blindfolded state.

Securely hidden in what was George's chamber, where he passed the first night of his captivity, they saw Sutoto with the offerings. Cinda took them, in silence, and disappeared, only to return instantly with the smoking viands.

"I call that quick work," said Harry.

"Yes, that's swift cooking," suggested George.

They ate in silence. "I wonder where the bridesmaid is who intends to make them talk?"

"Why don't you see her standing behind Cinda?"

"You mean the servant?"

"Of course."

This was almost too amusing for the boys. The rites were progressing very satisfactorily. Then Cinda removed the bandage, and an ineffable smile stole over Sutoto's features.

They commenced to talk. The maid said a few words, but the lovers paid no attention. The ceremony was going along just as-a perfect one should, when four stalwart warriors rushed in and seized Sutoto. Cinda knew who they were, and she sprang at them, as two seized her also.

One of them addressed a word to Sutoto, and then spoke to Cinda, and without further ceremony they were taken out through the open portal, and hurried to the ship.

The boys followed at a respectful distance, and when the pair had reached the deck the boys scrambled up, and hurriedly made their way to the large room, or cabin, where the Chief and the visitors were assembled, and which was brilliantly lighted for the occasion.

The criminals were brought before the Chief, who arose, and with a severe countenance began to upbraid Sutoto for his crime. Cinda meanwhile glanced around at the brilliant sight. She saw nothing to excite fear. Both were free from the warriors and stood there side by side, a handsome couple, as every one admitted.

Sutoto saw the boys. Just like boys are apt to be on such an occasion, they could not repress their laughter, although it was a silent exhibition of mirth. Then Sutoto knew, and so did Cinda, for she was not too much abashed to look up at Sutoto, while she leaned over and rested her head against him, and laid her hand on his arm.

Then the boys stopped laughing. There was nothing laughable about it now. It seemed too beautiful to laugh at, and when the great Chief went over, and rubbed his nose against Sutoto's every one knew that the compact was sealed.

I wish it were possible to describe the delight shown in the eyes of the bride and groom when they were led to the table containing the wedding gifts that came to them from Wonder Island.

"Oh! I am so sorry!" said Harry.

"Sorry for what? Yes, yes, I know now. We have nothing to give Sutoto, as our presents." And George said it with genuine grief.

Most of the articles exhibited were for the use of the bride, and designed for the home, of the new couple; but there was a fine array of the little trinkets which so delight the feminine heart.

The party sat down to the feast, with Sutoto and Cinda at one end of the table, while Mida presided at the other, the Chief being at her right, and his wife at her left.

For the first time in their lives they were to eat their food with knives and forks. They were adepts with the sharpened stick, which George had noted, and there was amusement at the many incidents that the new order brought forth.

"I remember," said George, "that the Professor told us the Italians, about the year 1700, were the first to use forks."

"Yes," replied John. "As late as the year 1800 the English did not use the fork, but the knife, for conveying food to the mouth; but the new-fangled idea, when once introduced, became universal, soon after that time; and it was then the custom for travelers to carry their own knives and forks when traveling."

The Professor said, addressing the Chief: "I am surprised that you use a fork at the table. While we do so universally, it was not originally our custom."

"I can remember," replied the Chief, "when it was not the habit to use any implement, but all were required to take food from the same dish with the hands. But at that time food was not served hot, but allowed to cool. But we found that the eating of hot articles became a custom, and then we had to use the pointed forks."

"I am curious to know what gives the roast such a beautiful flavor!" asked the Chief's wife. "I am told that you do not use leaves for flavoring."

"No," said Mida. "We now use spices, and the flavor is made more distinct by adding salt."

"What kinds of spices are used?"

"For meats, principally pepper, of which I have no doubt you have plenty on your island."

Of course, there was coffee, which grew in abundance in Wonder Island, and numerous trees of which had been discovered by the boys of the Chief's island. When this was brought out, and the natives first tasted it, there was some doubt on their part as to its food value.

Added interest was given to it when the Chief was induced to try it with a bountiful supply of cream and sugar. Then these articles attracted their attention.

"Is this a fruit?" he asked as a lump of sugar was handed him.

"No, it is made from cane, or from some vegetables."

"Made from vegetables? How can it be made from them? There is part of the flavor of fruit, but I cannot taste any vegetables in it."

Then the Professor explained that all fruit, as well as vegetables, had the same taste, and that they took out only that part and left the other.

"But what is this white liquid which you use in the new drink?"

"It is called 'cream,' and the cream is made from milk?"

"And what is milk made of?"

"It is taken from cows, a large animal, that people raise for that purpose."

As there was nothing on the island that was as large as a cow, or that resembled it in any manner, the Chief's curiosity was unbounded.

"I would like to see the animal from which this was obtained."

"But we have no animal with us."

"Then it never spoils?"

"Oh, yes, it will quickly grow sour and unpleasant if allowed to remain in a warm place."

He looked around in bewilderment, and the Professor seeing his embarrassment, continued: "In the ship we have a way to prevent the cream and the milk, as well, from spoiling. We will show you that."

Thus one article after the other called for some comment, and explanation. To the natives from Wonder Island this meal was an object lesson of only a few of the many things which they had learned from the white people.

But Sutoto and his bride could not be forgotten. When the meal was finished, the Professor arose, and said: "I have some news to impart to you. When the white people first came to Wonder Island, they found Uraso, and Muro, and they were the first to come to our aid against powerful tribes."

"One of their neighbors had at its head a wise Chief, Suros, known and respected by friend and foe alike, and he readily adopted the ideas of the white men, and offered his tribe to save us from destruction at the hands of those who were unfriendly."

"Sutoto was the nephew of the wise Chief Suros, and I have come to tell you that he is dead, and that we have been mourning for him."

Every one who glanced at Sutoto, saw that it greatly affected him. This address was translated to the Chief, by Uraso, as the Professor proceeded, the latter speaking it in such measured sentences, that it could be quickly grasped by the interpreter.

"We have all been sad, since his death, and we shall erect a suitable monument to his memory on our return."

The Chief looked at the Professor, and the latter instantly divined that he wanted some enlightenment.

"What does the white Chief mean by that?"

"It is the custom of the white man to put up something that all the people may look at, for years and years afterwards, so as to remind them that he has lived, and to tell the people what good he has done."

"And why should the people do that?"

"So as to teach people the example, and try to make them be good as he was."

"Do your people need to have such examples to make them do good?"

"That may not be necessary," replied the Professor, as he vainly tried to hide the smile that was trying to manifest itself.

"But do you not find it necessary to set the people a good example?" asked the Professor.

For a moment he looked around at the company in bewilderment, and he slowly replied: "No, I do not think it would do any good. If the people are bad, and they want to be bad, it will do them no good to tell them that I have always tried to do right."

There was a respectful silence, at this avowal, and the Professor continued: "There are many who think as you do, and we had one great teacher, called Confucius, who said: 'Do good not for the hope of reward, but because it is right.' Then we have also a precept which, interpreted, means: that happiness is in the heart."

"I do not know what that means," he replied.

"It means that the desire and the wish must come from within, and not from without." And the savage nodded an assent.

"But," continued the Professor, "I have some news to impart, that makes us all happy again. It is something that pertains to Sutoto, and I know you will all join in wishing him all happiness in the good fortune which Wonder Island brings to him, while this island is vying with us to make him happy."

What was this happy thing that the Professor portended? There was intense eagerness in the eyes of all who had left Wonder Island when the *Pioneer* sailed away, three weeks before.

"I want to present to you Sutoto, the new Chief of the Berees." The Professor could get no further. George and Harry were wild with excitement, and they bounded over to him and actually hugged him. Poor Cinda did not for the moment know what all this excitement meant.

She supposed that this was the white man's part of the ceremony, and quietly submitted. But she was quickly informed, and as she glanced at her father and mother, and the people came by and affectionately greeted them, she was so happy that tears actually flowed.

Then John came forward with a large box, which he carefully opened, and drew forth two packages, one of which he unwrapped, while Mida took the strings from the other.

"We want to present you these tokens, the presents of George and Harry. You are to wear these as an emblem of your authority." And George and Mida placed the most beautiful crown shaped hats on the heads of the couple.

"Is this part of the ceremony too?" asked Cinda, as she slyly glanced at Sutoto.

It is impossible to say who were the most surprised people,

the boys or Sutoto, since these presents had been prepared without their knowledge, and it atoned in a way for their neglect in not thinking of the gifts before.

But there were also other agreeable surprises in store for them. The wives of Uraso and Muro led Cinda to the table on which the presents were exposed, and also exhibited the many beautiful garments which had been prepared for her.

Her bewilderment was still greater when she was directed to turn, and found herself standing in front of a tall oval mirror which the boys had brought up, under the Professor's directions.

Her image in the mirror startled the bride beyond measure, and she innocently asked Sutoto whether this was also a part of the wedding ceremony.

According to the custom of the tribe, the couple had to go through the ordeal of the tribal dance, and when the boys learned of this they regretted that provision had not been made for the event. They were now in for everything which belonged to this unique wedding. The entire party broke up, and the boys regretted that the affair came to an end so soon.

As they filed down the steps and marched along the dock to the shore they noticed that the entire village was shining brightly with hundreds of the native candles, and everywhere were the well-known lamps, which the boys knew came from Wonder Island.

"What does all that mean?" asked Harry, as John came up.

"That means the dance, that is the final requirement of the wedding ceremony."

"But where are the dancers? Are we to take part?"

"Oh, no; no one who has partaken of the feast is permitted to take part."

"Well, that is certainly queer."

"Not more so than among many white people, where the dancers are those who have been specially selected for the purpose, and are professionals. In Biblical times the Jews had dancing as part of the religious ceremony, and that which took place in the Temple was participated in only by special ones set apart for that purpose."

No one was in sight, however, and the Chief led the entire company to a large green space, not far from his dwelling, and after a circle had been formed, they heard a peculiar humming sound, which seemed to be all about them, and this increased in intensity, and when at its height, two dozen or more of the native girls rushed in with a gliding, swaying motion, and circled around with peculiar grace, continuously giving forth the weird sounds that have been described.

It was intensely dramatic, and fascinated the boys. They had never seen anything so remarkable in its character, and for once they were unable to question its meaning, or ask for information concerning it.

For an hour this continued, until the boys thought the performers would certainly drop dead with fatigue; then, one after the other disappeared, and with each disappearance the sound of the humming grew less until but one remained. In some way, unknown to the boys she made the last circle around the green, bearing a wreath of leaves, and as she approached Sutoto and Cinda, wheeled about, and threw it over them.

"That is the final act," said John. "See, they are both within the wreath, and it signifies that they are bound together forever, even as the wreath, which has no end."

Roger Thompson Finlay

CHAPTER XVII

HUTOTON; THE PLACE OF DEATH

But the boys knew that they had some important things to attend to. The pleasures of life have an important part, but they were now engaged in serious work. The fact that they had accomplished so much was a great incentive to go on and investigate other things which were still mysteries, and which might be of great value to them.

The coming of the Professor had been a great pleasure to them. The developments of the past two weeks were ever in their minds and they could not repress the curiosity to visit the other islands, if such could be found.

Now that Sutoto was married they knew he would not be with them for a time, and they had not talked over the future plans. When, the next day, they and the Professor and John were together to consider the next step, it was with joy that the Professor informed them of the purpose of John to continue the investigations throughout that part of the ocean.

"It seems that your interpretation of Walter's note was entirely wrong," said John. "In any event it is certain that we are more than thirty leagues from Wonder Island, and not in the direction he pointed out."

"Then it is likely that if there is an island which will fit the place, it must be to the north," said Harry.

"That would be a natural conclusion," he answered. "It has occurred to me that the natural place for an island would be to the north."

The boys looked at him with surprise. "What makes you think so?" asked George.

"I judged so, merely from the conformation of this island."

"What is there in the island that makes you think so?"

"You have noticed that the island is very narrow east and west, and very much longer north and south."

"Yes; but that still does not make it plain to me."

"The island may be like the ridge of a mountain cropping out of the ocean. For instance, the Andes and the Sierras in the United States run north and south. Now suppose the ocean should cover the land, those mountains would form islands which would naturally be north and south of each other, and the islands themselves would be longer north and south than east and west."

"I see the idea. But we might find them to the south of this island, as well."

"Certainly; but as the northern section brings us nearer the supposed thirty leagues, we should, I think, make the investigation there first."

It was necessary that Sutoto should go back to Wonder Island. His position as Chief of the Berees made this essential. Furthermore, the age of the Professor made traveling and the hardships of investigating on foot a hard task, and besides it was necessary to take back the visitors.

"I have suggested to the Chief that we shall return, and have invited him to accompany us, and I am gratified to say that he has accepted. We shall, therefore, be ready to return within a few days," said the Professor.

"Have you said anything to him about the contemplated visit to Hutoton?" asked John.

"No; but I shall do so at once."

"Oh! that will give us an opportunity to take the paralytic back with us," suggested Harry.

"Yes; that will be the reason for our stopping there."

"Wouldn't it be a good idea to sail to the north, and investigate in that direction, on our way home?" remarked George.

"That has occurred to me."

The Chief gave careful instructions to his son, Calmo, in view of his proposed trip, and informed the Professor that he was anxious to accompany them at the earliest opportunity.

Two days thereafter, the entire party boarded the ship, and the course was set for the northern part of the island. There the Chief had the first opportunity to see the dreadful place where the criminals of his community had been sent.

There was no resentment on the part of the convicts. On the other hand, there was the most effusive welcome extended, and when the Chief saw the happiness and prosperity there, which he could not help but contrast with his own people, he was amazed.

The unfortunate patient was carefully taken to the ship, and during his removal did not in the least indicate by any sign that he knew what was going on about him.

John took many stores from the ship, and particularly garments, and articles of food for the people. All participated in the division, and the old man was delighted when he saw the gifts, the more so when John told him that they would soon be visited and other stores provided.

When the rolling motion of the boat was felt by the stricken man, he showed the first symptoms of consciousness. Sometimes he would look about him, and try to grasp something. On several occasions the Professor saw him open his eyes with a sort of questioning look.

But we cannot dwell too long on the result of the patient's progress, at this time. John felt, as did the Professor, that from that man they would be able to learn something, if he could ever regain his faculties. The boys gathered that much from the conversation, so that, for the present, he must be left to the tender care of the Professor, until later events are recorded.

From Hutoton the ship sailed directly north, it being understood that if no land was sighted before evening it would be useless to go farther in that direction. The *Pioneer* was a good sailer, and could easily, with a fair wind, make ten miles an hour, so they would have fully seven hours' run to test out their theory of land in that direction.

Before five o'clock John, who was constantly on the watch, came to the Professor and remarked that he believed the haze to the north indicated the presence of land. This was soon communicated to the boys, and there was no more idleness from that time on.

John's theory was correct. Slowly certain fixed objects appeared and some outlines that looked like mountains, and the boys could not repress their anxiety at the anticipated shore.

"Then we were right, after all," said Harry.

John smiled, as he replied: "I do not know; the calculations have not yet been made."

"I would like to know how our position can be found out from an examination of the sun," remarked George.

"That will require a long answer to explain fully but I shall try to answer it in a simple manner. The sailor takes an observation of the sun in two directions, namely, north and south, and east and west. You know, of course, that the sun moves north in the summer and south in the winter, and that the extreme southern point is in midwinter, Dec. 20: that in the spring, or March 20, it is directly above the equator, and in midsummer, or, on June 20, it is as far north as it can go."

"You mean," said George, "that it would be north of the equator."

"As we have the same calendar over the entire world, it is true everywhere. The difference is, of course, that summer and winter, and spring and autumn are reversed, north and south of the equator. All estimates as to locations are made by measuring angles."

"Then it must be something like surveying?"

"Yes; the same principles are applied. Here is a sketch, which shows the earth A, and B is the equatorial line. C is the position of the sun on September 20, or on June 20."

"Why are they in the same position on both days?"

"Yes; the sun crosses the equator September 20, on its way south, and then it again recrosses the equator coming north six months afterwards. On either of those days, if a person should stand at D, and look at the sun, there would be a line E, which projects out from the earth to the sun, and that is called the equatorial line."

"It is exactly at right angles to F, which passes through the poles. Now the drawing shows two other positions, namely G and H. These represent the extreme points of the travel of the sun north and south, or the positions that the sun occupy on Dec. 20, and June 20 of each year."

"I see," said Harry. "The points G and H are just 23 degrees north and south of the equator."

"That is correct, and there is another thing which can be learned from their positions."

"I know what it is."

"What?"

"It gives another line, or angle."

"So now we have two angles, this, and the equatorial line. Then, we know the exact distance of the sun from the earth, and this gives the first measurement, and with the angle formed by the line I, taken in connection with the line E, it is easy to determine just where, or how far the sun is to the north or to the south, and if you did not, for instance, know the time of the year, a man could by such a measurement, tell, by the angle thus formed, the exact date."

"I understand that now," remarked George. "The sailor, in getting the angle, simply measures that, and if he knows where the sun is on that day he will then have two angles, one that he knows beforehand, and the other that he finds out by looking at the sun."

"That is correct. The Nautical Chart gives all that information, so that it saves a large amount of work in making the calculations."

"That gives the way to determine positions north and south. But how about east and west?"

"In the same manner exactly so far as the angle measurements are concerned, but in this case, instead of taking the time, in days or in months, as in reckoning north and south, we must take time in minutes, and to do that the entire globe is laid off in minutes and degrees, which the nautical tables give, and the mariner knows when he obtains a certain angle just how far east or west he is located by the chart."

"But if he has no chart?"

"Then he must figure out the position for himself, which he can do if he has what is called Greenwich, or standard time, and has, also the correct time of the day where his ship is."

Land was beyond; there was no question of that. It rose out of the water higher than the island they had just left, which the boys had named *Venture* Island.

The Chief knew nothing of the land before them. He had told

John that years before he learned that there was a land where there were many bad people, who killed and ate each other, but he did not know the exact direction.

The vessel was sailed along the coast, and the field glasses were used to scan the land. It had the appearance of the other islands which they now knew. Vegetation was magnificent, and growing everywhere, but there was not the sign of a habitation anywhere.

After an hour's sail they rounded a point, and beyond was the first cove, or indentation along the coast. To that John directed the course of the vessel, and they ran in very close, since he knew from the abrupt sloping beach that it must be a deep bay.

The men could scarcely man the boat quickly enough. A dozen of them, together with John, Muro and Uraso, took the first boat, while a second boat was filled with the warriors who also were accompanied by some of the natives of Venture island.

The Professor and the others remained on board, while the party made the preliminary examinations of the immediate neighborhood. John formed two parties, one under command of Muro, and the other of Uraso. The boys were with Uraso, while he was with Muro. The object was to find out as quickly as possible what they would have to meet, and the result would enable them to determine the future plans.

"It is understood, now," remarked John, "that the two exploring parties shall take the two courses outlined, Muro and his men, to go directly east, while Uraso will take a course to the northeast, and proceed in that direction for three hours, and then the two parties are to turn toward each other, and mutually report. This will give us an opportunity to find out something, unless the island is a very large one, and requires subsequent exploration to ascertain whether it is inhabited."

John had purposely selected the route to the east, as he saw the high elevation in that direction, and George laughed, as he said, slyly: "John is still after the caves," and Harry laughed, as he recalled the keenness with which John had arranged the trips.

John did make his way to the highest points, and soon learned, from the observations, that the island was inhabited, but the trip of the boys was more exciting, so we shall more particularly detail their adventures.

Before they had gone two hours evidences grew thick and fast that tribes inhabited the island. Muro, and the different men, were continually finding traces, none of them, however, which indicated that the people were near at hand, or that the telltale marks had been recently made.

But now signs began to be apparent to the boys also; the bones of animals, lying around the spot where a fire had been gave them the first real sensation. Muro glanced at the boys, and at some bones, and the action on his part was so peculiar, that George quietly remarked:

"Muro looked so peculiarly at me when I glanced at the bones, over there, that I wonder what he meant?"

"I saw it too," answered Harry. "Let us have another look at them;" and acting on the suggestion they went over. Muro followed. They did not appear to pay any attention to him; but he was quick to join them, and as he did so he slowly nodded his head.

"Are they human remains?" said Harry, as he turned to Muro, questioningly.

"Yes; and this is not the first we have seen," he answered. "We may find them now at any time. I am now sure that there are several tribes here."

"What makes you believe so?"

"Because we have found different kinds of hair, which is usually the best evidence of the differences in the tribes, as each has its own peculiarity."

"Savages, and cannibals!" said George reflectively.

"But we must go on. We have still an hour in this direction before we turn to the south and east," said Harry.

There was more caution now exercised, and the speed was accordingly reduced, in view of the especial care which they took. In order to understand what happened the reader should know something of the nature of the country.

Some places in Wonder Island had the same sort of timber and undergrowth, and they went through some dense forests, in which vines and small brush made traveling difficult. They had to cut their way through some of this vegetation.

The land was not low or flat. If it had been there would have been a dense jungle. Sometimes they passed through half-grown forests, and these places were the most difficult to scour, because an enemy might be within fifty feet, and not be discovered.

It was in just such a place that they received their first surprise; a shower of arrows, so thick that they instantly knew it could not have been made by only a dozen or so. Some of the arrows found their marks, and two of the men sank down, while Muro coolly drew one of the crude missiles from his arm.

"Drop down!" cried Muro.

There was not a savage in sight; still a number of arrows fell around them. "Remain quiet, and I will find them?" said Muro, as he crept forward quietly through the dense grass.

George and Harry followed, although it was evident it was not Muro's wish. Before they had gone ten feet, Muro turned, and pointed ahead. "They are there; at least one party. Get ready for a shot."

The savages, noting the quiet in their front, now cautiously peered through the bush, and the boys saw the most hideous countenances. "We might give them a round," said Muro, and after carefully aiming, the guns spoke.

The simultaneous explosion of the three guns, raised pandemonium on all sides. They were now surrounded by at least a hundred of the savages, but for some reason the little party of twenty awed them, and instead of making a charge, they rushed toward the place where the three victims of the gunshots lay.

Muro's arm was bleeding profusely, and George quickly bound it up, while the enemy were hesitating. "Do not shoot, unless they rush at us. I will talk: to them, and try to get an understanding."

Then, in a loud voice Muro called to them, saying they were friends, and not enemies. There was no response. Thinking that they knew nothing of the dialect, he tried another, and the only response was the evident determination of the savages to attack again.

The boys and Muro could plainly hear their chattering, but the latter said that what they were saying was not intelligible to him, and that they must now prepare for a fight.

"Get your guns ready, and be prepared for a charge. If they come so close that you cannot use the guns, then we must be prepared to meet them with our knives, and we must all stand together, and not become separated."

Instead of attacking, however, there was silence, after the first excitement. "They are trying to find, out what struck their comrades when we fired," remarked Muro.

"Yes; I think it was a big surprise."

"I recall," continued Muro, "when we had our first brush with you that we could not find the arrow which we supposed was made by your bullet. That frightened us more than anything else."

There was not the slightest movement on the part of an enemy for a full half hour. This is the most trying sort of tactics. If you can see the enemy, or note that he is doing something, there is some relief to the tension, but where he can neither be seen, nor heard, it tries the nerves of the strongest man.

Muro knew that this inactivity on the part of the savages had its purpose. Probably, they intended to remain there until night, and overwhelm them in the rush. Muro had other plans, however.

"We cannot remain here. We must make the attack. Remain

here, and permit me to feel out their positions, and also to determine what they are doing." He glided away from them noiselessly, and how he kept the tall grass and weeds from swaying, the boys could not determine at that time.

It did not take Muro long to see the situation. They were surrounded by a cordon of savages, and while spying, saw a new lot of them coming up. The plan was plain enough, and it meant a fight now, or a night defense.

When he returned, he had his plans formed. "They are being reinforced, and we have, probably, a hundred and fifty, or more, around us. John is, no doubt, too far away to come to our assistance, and our only hope is to attack them now, so we might as well take the necessary steps."

While on his investigations Muro had discovered a fallen tree, which was not more than fifty feet to their left. "We must reach that tree, and by digging a shallow trench at one side, can easily defend ourselves, as well as pick them off at our leisure."

Slowly they moved, in crawling attitudes, toward the place indicated. The tree was not a large one, but it made an admirable breastworks, and with their knives each man dug out a shallow hole, piling up the earth beyond the hole, so as to shelter them from the arrows, which they knew would be rained on them.

This work required a full half hour, and when it was completed, and Muro had satisfied himself that each one was supplied with sufficient ammunition, he was ready for the second stage of the game.

"We must attract them, by some form of action. I will take three with me, and crawl forward, until we can catch glimpse of some of the watchers. Those we will attack, and then fall back, and do the same on the other sides."

Muro indicated those who were to follow, and after going only a short distance the boys heard the shots, then four more. This brought the sounds of voices from every direction. Muro and his men, during the excitement, crawled to another portion of the line, and repeated the manoeuver.

This, for the moment threw them into consternation, but they quickly rallied, and now it was plain that they were pressing forward to rush the position occupied by the boys. It was now obvious that the precaution of making the defensive position, as Muro had suggested, was their only salvation.

CHAPTER XVIII

DISCOVERY OF A NEW ISLAND, AND A SAVAGE TRIBE

Nothing could describe the uproar that the second volley created in the ranks of the besiegers. Yell after yell came from the hundreds of throats that were about them. It was now war to the end. There could be no compromise.

While the boys had been in many difficult and trying experiences before, this was the first time that they grew pale, and had strong misgivings. They knew, however, that the object of the shrieks and yells of savages were for the purpose of driving terror into the hearts of their foes.

In this respect it might not thus affect them, but when they considered the overwhelming numbers around them, we cannot blame them for feeling alarmed.

They were coming forward, and on all sides. "Remember, what John used to tell us: it is the shots that hit which count. Fire deliberately, and keep together. Do not use your revolvers until they are close, and you cannot use the guns."

Closer and closer they came, and Muro and the men were silent. "Now, get ready! Shoot deliberately!"

The first salvo was fired. It was a staggering blow. They reloaded, while the enemy was trying to recover, and the second volley belched forth.

Then, when the execution was noticed, and they saw their people fall all about them, they charged forward in one mass, and the boys looked at each other, for a moment, and George reached over and gave Harry's hand one pressure, and then turned away and began to fire as fast as he could aim the weapon.

They were still coming on. The demons were nearly up to the log. For some reason the savages did not heed those who fell. It had not struck terror into their hearts, as the boys hoped. How would this end? The enemy was now too close to make their guns of any use. The revolvers were drawn, and the cracks from them became almost a continuous roar.

They were still coming. Soon the ammunition would be gone. The boys realized this. They were determined to die fighting, and they began to feel for their knives which must be the final act in the great tragedy.

Then they heard something louder than the cracks of their own weapons and the shrieks of the devils around them. Some one was shooting. They could see the startled faces of the savages, as they turned and swung around. The attack ceased, and Muro sprang up on the log, with a yell.

Could he be mad? The boys were stupefied. "Come on!" cried Muro. "Here is John!"

This announcement, coming at an unexpected moment, was such a reaction to the poor boys, that they could hardly raise themselves. Another volley; they could hear it now. There was another yell from the savages, and then they could be seen rushing through the brush.

The men with John ran up, and John struggled forward through the weeds. "Are you hurt?" asked John, as he sprang to the side of the boys.

"No! no!" cried George, and he fell down, overcome with the excitement, while Harry could not speak for a moment.

"That was a close call," said John. "We heard the first shots an hour ago, and we turned to take this direction. Then we heard nothing for a long time, and as we were coming over the hill beyond the firing commenced but we could see nothing, so we hurried forward and soon saw the smoke, and then the savages coming from the bush, and directly to the east we noticed fifty or more coming this way, but they are not here yet."

"I wonder how many attacked us?" asked George.

"It is difficult to tell, but it is safe to say that there were at least two hundred in the fight. Oh, no; the boys will not follow them up very far," said John, as Harry looked apprehensively toward the direction that John's men were going.

He blew the whistle, and gradually the men straggled in, reporting that the savages appeared terror-stricken, as they had had no idea that there was another force in the neighborhood, and they did not stop to consider the possible number.

"I am sorry for these poor people," remarked John. "We must hunt up the wounded."

Searchers were set to work, and the wounded, when found, were carried to an open place beyond, and their hurts examined and bandaged. At first terror showed itself on their faces, but as John and Muro, together with the boys, washed their wounds, and wrapped bandages around the limbs, they lay there and marveled at the actions of their enemies.

More than two dozen had been killed, and forty-two wounded, nearly all in the legs or bodies, those having arm wounds being enabled to get away.

On Muro's orders a watch was set on the movements of the savages, and from time to time reports were brought in concerning them. They had retreated eastwardly, and were now off less than a half mile, where they were assembled, and evidently debating the situation.

John and Muro well knew that their present force, now numbering forty-one, and all well armed, would be more than a match for the savage force, still, it would not be advisable to prolong the explorations for the day, as it was desirable to report the situation of affairs to the Professor.

After making the sufferers comfortable they started on the march back to the ship. During the period while caring for the wounded, John and Muro tried to engage the savages in conversation but all attempts to learn their language failed, and, as they were about to leave, John said to Muro:

"Do you think that man is a chief?"

"I know he is; I spotted him from the first, and saw from his actions, and the fact of his being obeyed, that he was a man of some authority."

"I agree with you," said Uraso, "that he is the one we must take with us."

A litter was quickly improvised and the savage gently laid on, and with this, as their only encumbrance, they started for the return march. Five of the men had been wounded, all in the arms and body, and none of them dangerously, so that there was no trouble in the march.

They filed out to the west, avoiding as much exposure as possible. Muro's men had been on the observing line, and at Muro's suggestion they occasionally showed themselves, so as to assure the natives that they were still holding their ground.

As the two forces were starting for the ship, Muro prepared a decoy, so that the savages could see what appeared to be two figures. Then he hurriedly told John what he had done, and the march began, as rapidly as possible, at first, and a rear guard was provided to watch the movements of their enemies.

Two miles beyond the scene of the fight the party halted, and George was assisted to climb a tree, from which point they might be seen.

"I can see them plainly," he called down. "They are now around the wounded. I cannot see what they are doing, but there is a big crowd."

He waited for some time, and then cried out: "I believe they are coming this way. I think it is time for us to be moving." And George slipped down, as John gave the order to go on.

The rear guard, with John and Uraso, were now following up behind the marchers. "Go on, without stopping," he said, as they took up their positions.

The boys begged to be permitted to remain with the rear

guard, but John refused to have them exposed. In an hour and a half they ascended an elevation from which the ship could be seen in the bay to the southwest.

During that time only once had the runner returned from John to notify them of the progress of the natives. The last information, therefore, was about a half hour before, and it was now obvious that the savages were determined to follow them up, and this would bring them within view of the vessel.

Before descending the last declivity that led to the beach, John and the Chief appeared, and told the boys that all of the tribe was behind them, and that the cause of the pursuit was, unquestionably, to recover the Chief who had been taken along.

At the suggestion of John three shots were fired to attract the attention of those on the boat, while several of the fleetest runners speeded down the beach and quickly advised the Professor of the situation.

Two boat loads of warriors were quickly sent to shore, and when John and the party with him came up to the beach, the savages had reached the crest of the hill, and ranged up in line, but halted to witness the spectacle before them.

The wounded chief was taken to the vessel, and the Professor immediately gave him the best care, but he remarked: "This man is desperately wounded, and will require the best of attention to enable him to pull through."

All the men were finally placed on board, and their experiences related. An immediate consultation was held. John and the boys insisted on remaining with a sufficient force to enable them to carry out their explorations, but the

Professor seemed to oppose it.

"I quite agree with you that, from what John has said, there are reasons aside from the cannibals over there, why we should explore it from one end to the other."

The boys cast a side glance at John. Did John find something that made him so insistent to remain? They repressed their curiosity, however, for the time. To their minds they thought the natives were the incentive, notwithstanding the terrible fight they had just engaged in, although they were willing to take the risk.

But it was finally settled. John was to have the force now on board, and he, with the boys, was to explore, and, if need be, to conquer the natives on the island. The *Pioneer* would, in the meantime, sail to Wonder Island, and return with food and ammunition, and reinforcements.

There was thus left at their disposal fifty-five men, with a fair supply of ammunition. Uraso and Muro were to be of the party, as events just related showed that there was serious work to do before they might be able to return.

That night, while making the final arrangements on the vessel, the boys sought John, and asked him more particularly concerning his trip.

"We have had no opportunity to speak to you, but the Professor said you had learned enough about the island to determine you to explore it fully," said George.

"That is true. I have found what I believe to be the identical spot described in the charts, and I have found the solution, I think, of Walter's note and of the skull."

This was, indeed, something of importance to them, but John informed them that for certain reasons it might be better to defer the explanation until they had made the final explorations.

The boys knew he must have some pretty good reason for thus explaining and laying the matter before them, and they forebore further questionings.

The next morning, when all the supplies and ammunition had been taken off, and the final good-byes were said, the party stood on the shore while the *Pioneer* slowly moved out, and was soon racing before the wind on its way to Wonder Island.

A council was held before they attempted to march into the interior. "I have every reason to believe that the band which we met yesterday is in the immediate vicinity, and that they have been watching our movements," remarked John.

"In that case," remarked Uraso, "I favor the route to the east, which, while it may offer us still greater obstacles, in view of our observations there, still it might enable us the more quickly to overcome the tribe we have just met."

The boys looked at each other significantly. "I wonder what Uraso can be talking about? There must be something very much out of the usual, in the eastern part of the island."

"I am interested in knowing what he means by 'the observation' they made there," responded Harry.

CHAPTER XIX

FIGHT WITH NATIVES
AND RETURN TO WONDER ISLAND

When the *Pioneer* sailed for Unity it was with the understanding that she was to return within a week or ten days. At a cliff in the headland, which jutted out on the southern side of the bay, a sort of post office station was established, because if the ship should return while they were in the interior, it would be well for the commander of the *Pioneer* to know where to go in the event that the eastern or the northern coast should be much more convenient for John and his party.

It was nearly a hundred miles from the Island to Wonder Island, and there would be no occasion for the Professor to hurry back a relief, except to supply additional ammunition, because they did not for an instant expect to meet a tribe that would give them such a fight.

There was still enough to provide, probably five rounds per man, so that it made them a pretty respectable fighting force. The weather was such that the force on the island did not require tents for shelter, and with the native fruits the party could well subsist for quite a time without assistance.

It was agreed that the party should keep together, and no straggling be permitted, as it was evident they had a very bitter foe to deal with. The severely wounded Chief, who was taken along, was under the personal charge of the Professor, the understanding being that as soon as his wounds were satisfactorily progressing, an effort would be made to open up communication with him, and through that channel they could reach the inhabitants of the island, and thus advise them that they did not mean to do them an injury.

"I wonder if that isn't the real reason why John does not want to go for the fellows who attacked us," asked George.

"That may be so. It never occurred to me before. It seems to me, though," answered Harry, "that they will get but little out of that fellow in a week's time. You know they are very much reserved at times."

"Or stubborn," suggested George.

One of the things that John was careful about related to the organization of the force, so that it would at all times be ready for action. In order to carry out this idea and make it effectual, he divided the fighters into two squads of twenty-five men each, under the commands of Uraso and Muro, the arrangement being such that one squad should have charge of the patrolling and picketing for a period of two days, and then the other should take charge for a like time.

There was always the most perfect accord between the two Chiefs, and John wisely allowed them to arrange those matters in such a way as would be most satisfactory to them.

Before noon the following day the force marched out from Security Harbor, as they had named the bay, and took up the trail made by John and his party two days before.

"We have names for the two islands, and for about all the principal points, but we have no name for this place," said Harry, as they were marching along.

"Quite true," answered George, reflectively. Then, with a laugh, he said: "As they have cannibals here, according to the evidence so far gathered, I think *Maneta* would be a name that would tell the story about as well as anything." And George laughed as he made the suggestion.

He was an adept in applying names, being generally the first to make suggestions in that direction, and he was rarely at a loss for an apt designation.

The route was over a country which was rich in vegetation. During the first ten miles the ascent was gradual, and the fruit and nuts were abundant, while new species of trees and flowers attracted the boys.

"Harry and I have found a plant that has flies and other insects all over the leaves, and I believe it actually catches and holds. Here is a sample," said George, as he presented a branch to John.

John examined it carefully. Then he said: "This is a plant of which we have several in the United States, but none which are as active. This is called Venus' Fly Trap."

"That is curious," remarked Harry. "I wouldn't have paid any attention to it but I saw a fly alight on it, and these little feelers seemed to close around it, and hold it."

"It works on that plan exactly. It is in that way it gets its food."

"But why should the feelers be able to grasp the fly the

moment it touches the leaf?"

"Do you recall about what the Professor told you of the peculiar power of plants to absorb food of particular kinds by a faculty called *irritability*?"

"Yes; I remember."

"By means of that, plants are enabled to select just the kinds of substances that they want, and can digest. If you will carefully notice the leaf, after it has seized a fly it will be observed that the leaf exudes a watery substance, and that has the property of digesting the fly, or of converting the liquid part of the insect into a form of food which is taken through the leaf, and from the leaf it goes into the plant itself."

"I thought plants got their food from the roots only?"

"Leaves are just the same as roots. They are terminals, and moisture as well as foods, such, for instance, as nitrogen, is absorbed and fed to the plant through the leaves."

As they progressed they could see evidences of human occupation, and in many places the remains of fire. It was while making a detour from the regular route taken by John that they saw the first startling thing.

It was found at a place where a rude hut was discovered in a dilapidated condition. Directly behind the hut was a raised sort of dais, supported on two posts, and this was filled with human skulls, all in an advanced stage of decay.

It was noticed only by accident, as the area around the hut was thickly grown up by the vegetation. The boys were naturally startled at the sight.

"What does that mean?" asked Harry.

John replied: "This is evidence that the people here are head hunters."

"What do you mean by *head hunters*?"

"Certain savages have the belief that their importance depends on the number of heads they can capture."

"Where do they get them?"

"It is necessary for them to kill their enemies, and impale the heads, or nail them up to their huts."

"Is it a religious ceremony?"

"In some cases that is so. In some tribes the object is merely to show bravery and manliness. The more heads a man possesses the braver he is."

The vicinity of the hut was carefully examined, and Uraso brought to John a very curiously arranged shell, with a handle to it. It was, in fact, a rattle. John took the article, and after examining it for some time, remarked:

"These people will be difficult to deal with; very difficult."

"Why do you form that conclusion from the examination of the rattle?"

"This is a vele."

"A *vele*; and what in the world is that?"

"A vele is a sort of hoodoo; it is something that many natives believe in with such tenacity that if any one having this rattle points to him and declares him veleed, and announces that the veleed one will die the next day, he will lay down and actually expire as predicted."

"Do you believe such tales?" asked Harry.

"Of course those stories are hard to understand, but the missionaries on the Melanesian Islands vouch for many things similar to that. In 1871, Bishop Patterson, one of the missionaries, was murdered by the natives of those islands, and many of the facts in regard to their customs were then established."

"But how do they work the vele?"

"The place where the vele is worked to the most unlimited extent is in the Island of Guadalcaner, one of the Solomon Islands, although it has its counterpart in many other places. The vele rattler is carefully kept in a bamboo box, and when the owner wishes to destroy an enemy he takes the vele, and searches for him.

"In doing so he must not be seen by any one. If he is seen the vele will not be effective. When he finds his enemy the vele is pointed to the man, and the rattles shaken, and while doing so the one exorcising the spell must turn his face away and utter curses. As soon as his enemy hears this, he turns to see who has veleed him, and he then glances around to see if any one has seen the vele."

"Are you sure that the rattle is for that purpose?"

"There is no question of it, and it is an evidence that the natives are intensely superstitious, and such people are very difficult to deal with."

"I suppose we shall have witch doctors to deal with here?" asked George.

"That is a very natural supposition."

"Did you see some of these things when you came over here yesterday?"

"Yes."

It was evident to both boys that they were going direct to the mountains, and the general character of the surroundings reminded them so much of the mountains on Wonder Island, that they felt assured John would be able to find the cave for which he was searching.

That night they encamped on a small stream which was, no doubt, formed by a spring, as its waters were deliciously cool, and refreshing.

During that night, shortly after twelve o'clock, the boys heard the most peculiar noises, like a doleful, continuous cry, echoed and reechoed from hill to mountain,—something indescribable, but they refrained from saying anything to John about it.

Some of the boys who were present and heard it were singularly affected, and it must be said that the boys themselves, notwithstanding the experiences they had passed through, were not altogether composed in their minds.

When Uraso and Muro appeared next morning, after a night of scouting, they were startled by the accounts which were furnished, as to the number and warlike character of the inhabitants, and a council was held to decide whether it would be advisable to proceed with their limited force.

If they knew, beyond question, that the island was occupied by another tribe, it might enable them to make peace with one of them, and thus pave the way for approaching these people.

It was unfortunate that the first contact with the natives brought them into open hostilities, much as they desired to avoid it, but it was too late now.

"From your investigations," said John, addressing the two chiefs, "can you give any idea of the number of natives in this tribe?"

"We were unable to get near the village, but during the night we touched three different parties, one over by the high ridge, one a mile to the front, and the other over in the open ground not far from the place we had the fight. If I can judge anything by that I should say they have a number of warriors," answered Uraso.

"That does, indeed, look as though they are ready to meet us from whatever direction we may attack them," remarked John.

"The thing which is the most singular to me," remarked Muro, "is the way they are coming at us after the fight over there. If they were a weak lot they would draw off, and keep away from us, and that makes me think they have a lot of warriors, and are simply waiting until they can collect all of them."

"We must do one of two things," ventured John, on reflection. "Either to go on with the men we have, or to wait until the *Pioneer* returns, and then go back with her and fit out a force of ample size to meet them. It is our wish to win over the people by peaceful means, but our weakness may be the worst possible way of accomplishing that purpose."

Uraso and Muro were both in favor of returning and waiting for the *Pioneer*, as they knew it would be likely to show up within the next three days, and their views decided the matter.

"Under the circumstances we must leave this place before it is too late in the day, or we may have trouble in reaching the landing, although we can easily hold them off with our rifles, but we must avoid bloodshed," and on this point John was insistent.

The camp was astir and all the equipment in hand within fifteen minutes, although they had not yet partaken of breakfast. Uraso took the first turn, as commander of the rear guard, while the main body hurried on to cross the valley, before the savages could get the first notice of the retirement.

Notwithstanding the great caution displayed, several shots were heard before the slope on the other side was reached, and they knew that Uraso was engaged.

It is difficult, sometimes, to know just how information travels among savage people, but in this case, the peculiar beatings of the drums which could be heard in the dim distance, was sufficient to satisfy Muro that they had watchers, and a signaling means from treetops and from the crests of the great hills all around them.

An hour afterwards Uraso's men were seen in the distance, and, although they had fired no more shots, it was evident that the natives were now in force and pressing against him with all their might. Only the consummate skill of Uraso prevented them from rushing the men under his command.

But the top of the hill was reached; the landing was not much more than a mile beyond that, and John hurriedly took a half dozen men, and George and Harry with him, in order to select the final line of defense within reach of the landing place, while Uraso and Muro held them in check.

The boys were ahead of the little party, swinging along and trying to get to the elevated point which John indicated as the most available place, when two powerful natives sprang across their path, and before either could draw a weapon, they were pounced upon and seized by two more who approached from the rear.

With great presence of mind Harry cocked and fired the gun which his captors were struggling for. The shot went through the arm of the native who had seized George, and the latter, now free, raised his rifle and brought it down with all force on the nearest one.

John and the men with him needed no further information as to the situation. They were practically surrounded. That was his first thought; but, as no more natives appeared, and the two remaining savages started on a run it began to be evident that they were only scouts who expected an easy capture of the two boys.

There was no more straggling or running ahead after that. Uraso and the rear guard came up with a rush on hearing the shots, but were reassured when they saw the party intact.

The heights were gained, and before they could arrange for the defense the natives appeared from three quarters, and held off a quarter of a mile beyond.

During the following day John tried to establish communications with the natives, but they rebuffed all efforts, and the arrival of the *Pioneer* was anxiously awaited.

On the third day the natives were observed closer at various points, and they began to grow bolder, but at noon of the fourth day the sharp eyes of Muro discovered the glimpse of a sail to the west.

Within two hours the form of the ship could be seen. The *Pioneer* was making for the landing, and a cheer went up from the men at the welcome sight.

There was not much difficulty in descending the cliffs and establishing communications with the vessel, and within an hour they were aboard and the natives could plainly be seen coming down the opposite slope waving defiance to the ship.

The next day the *Pioneer* sailed up Enterprise River. The people in Unity were anxious to learn of the new island, and to hear of the exploits with the savage tribe which the boys had encountered.

"The Treasures of the Islands," the next book in this series, relates the further experiences of the boys upon their return to Rescue Island.

THE END

Choose from Thousands of 1stWorldLibrary Classics By

A. M. Barnard
Ada Leverson
Adolphus William Ward
Aesop
Agatha Christie
Alexander Aaronsohn
Alexander Kielland
Alexandre Dumas
Alfred Gatty
Alfred Ollivant
Alice Duer Miller
Alice Turner Curtis
Alice Dunbar
Allen Chapman
Alleyne Ireland
Ambrose Bierce
Amelia E. Barr
Amory H. Bradford
Andrew Lang
Andrew McFarland Davis
Andy Adams
Angela Brazil
Anna Alice Chapin
Anna Sewell
Annie Besant
Annie Hamilton Donnell
Annie Payson Call
Annie Roe Carr
Annonaymous
Anton Chekhov
Archibald Lee Fletcher
Arnold Bennett
Arthur C. Benson
Arthur Conan Doyle
Arthur M. Winfield
Arthur Ransome
Arthur Schnitzler
Arthur Train
Atticus
B.H. Baden-Powell
B. M. Bower
B. C. Chatterjee
Baroness Emmuska Orczy
Baroness Orczy
Basil King
Bayard Taylor
Ben Macomber
Bertha Muzzy Bower
Bjornstjerne Bjornson

Booth Tarkington
Boyd Cable
Bram Stoker
C. Collodi
C. E. Orr
C. M. Ingleby
Carolyn Wells
Catherine Parr Traill
Charles A. Eastman
Charles Amory Beach
Charles Dickens
Charles Dudley Warner
Charles Farrar Browne
Charles Ives
Charles Kingsley
Charles Klein
Charles Hanson Towne
Charles Lathrop Pack
Charles Romyn Dake
Charles Whibley
Charles Willing Beale
Charlotte M. Braeme
Charlotte M. Yonge
Charlotte Perkins Stetson
Clair W. Hayes
Clarence Day Jr.
Clarence E. Mulford
Clemence Housman
Confucius
Coningsby Dawson
Cornelis DeWitt Wilcox
Cyril Burleigh
D. H. Lawrence
Daniel Defoe
David Garnett
Dinah Craik
Don Carlos Janes
Donald Keyhoe
Dorothy Kilner
Dougan Clark
Douglas Fairbanks
E. Nesbit
E. P. Roe
E. Phillips Oppenheim
E. S. Brooks
Earl Barnes
Edgar Rice Burroughs
Edith Van Dyne
Edith Wharton

Edward Everett Hale
Edward J. O'Biren
Edward S. Ellis
Edwin L. Arnold
Eleanor Atkins
Eleanor Hallowell Abbott
Eliot Gregory
Elizabeth Gaskell
Elizabeth McCracken
Elizabeth Von Arnim
Ellem Key
Emerson Hough
Emilie F. Carlen
Emily Bronte
Emily Dickinson
Enid Bagnold
Enilor Macartney Lane
Erasmus W. Jones
Ernie Howard Pie
Ethel May Dell
Ethel Turner
Ethel Watts Mumford
Eugene Sue
Eugenie Foa
Eugene Wood
Eustace Hale Ball
Evelyn Everett-green
Everard Cotes
F. H. Cheley
F. J. Cross
F. Marion Crawford
Fannie E. Newberry
Federick Austin Ogg
Ferdinand Ossendowski
Fergus Hume
Florence A. Kilpatrick
Fremont B. Deering
Francis Bacon
Francis Darwin
Frances Hodgson Burnett
Frances Parkinson Keyes
Frank Gee Patchin
Frank Harris
Frank Jewett Mather
Frank L. Packard
Frank V. Webster
Frederic Stewart Isham
Frederick Trevor Hill
Frederick Winslow Taylor

Friedrich Kerst
Friedrich Nietzsche
Fyodor Dostoyevsky
G.A. Henty
G.K. Chesterton
Gabrielle E. Jackson
Garrett P. Serviss
Gaston Leroux
George A. Warren
George Ade
Geroge Bernard Shaw
George Cary Eggleston
George Durston
George Ebers
George Eliot
George Gissing
George MacDonald
George Meredith
George Orwell
George Sylvester Viereck
George Tucker
George W. Cable
George Wharton James
Gertrude Atherton
Gordon Casserly
Grace E. King
Grace Gallatin
Grace Greenwood
Grant Allen
Guillermo A. Sherwell
Gulielma Zollinger
Gustav Flaubert
H. A. Cody
H. B. Irving
H. C. Bailey
H. G. Wells
H. H. Munro
H. Irving Hancock
H. R. Naylor
H. Rider Haggard
H. W. C. Davis
Haldeman Julius
Hall Caine
Hamilton Wright Mabie
Hans Christian Andersen
Harold Avery
Harold McGrath
Harriet Beecher Stowe
Harry Castlemon
Harry Coghill
Harry Houidini

Hayden Carruth
Helent Hunt Jackson
Helen Nicolay
Hendrik Conscience
Hendy David Thoreau
Henri Barbusse
Henrik Ibsen
Henry Adams
Henry Ford
Henry Frost
Henry James
Henry Jones Ford
Henry Seton Merriman
Henry W Longfellow
Herbert A. Giles
Herbert Carter
Herbert N. Casson
Herman Hesse
Hildegard G. Frey
Homer
Honore De Balzac
Horace B. Day
Horace Walpole
Horatio Alger Jr.
Howard Pyle
Howard R. Garis
Hugh Lofting
Hugh Walpole
Humphry Ward
Ian Maclaren
Inez Haynes Gillmore
Irving Bacheller
Isabel Cecilia Williams
Isabel Hornibrook
Israel Abrahams
Ivan Turgenev
J. G.Austin
J. Henri Fabre
J. M. Barrie
J. M. Walsh
J. Macdonald Oxley
J. R. Miller
J. S. Fletcher
J. S. Knowles
J. Storer Clouston
J. W. Duffield
Jack London
Jacob Abbott
James Allen
James Andrews
James Baldwin

James Branch Cabell
James DeMille
James Joyce
James Lane Allen
James Lane Allen
James Oliver Curwood
James Oppenheim
James Otis
James R. Driscoll
Jane Abbott
Jane Austen
Jane L. Stewart
Janet Aldridge
Jens Peter Jacobsen
Jerome K. Jerome
Jessie Graham Flower
John Buchan
John Burroughs
John Cournos
John F. Kennedy
John Gay
John Glasworthy
John Habberton
John Joy Bell
John Kendrick Bangs
John Milton
John Philip Sousa
John Taintor Foote
Jonas Lauritz Idemil Lie
Jonathan Swift
Joseph A. Altsheler
Joseph Carey
Joseph Conrad
Joseph E. Badger Jr
Joseph Hergesheimer
Joseph Jacobs
Jules Vernes
Julian Hawthrone
Julie A Lippmann
Justin Huntly McCarthy
Kakuzo Okakura
Karle Wilson Baker
Kate Chopin
Kenneth Grahame
Kenneth McGaffey
Kate Langley Bosher
Kate Langley Bosher
Katherine Cecil Thurston
Katherine Stokes
L. A. Abbot
L. T. Meade

L. Frank Baum
Latta Griswold
Laura Dent Crane
Laura Lee Hope
Laurence Housman
Lawrence Beasley
Leo Tolstoy
Leonid Andreyev
Lewis Carroll
Lewis Sperry Chafer
Lilian Bell
Lloyd Osbourne
Louis Hughes
Louis Joseph Vance
Louis Tracy
Louisa May Alcott
Lucy Fitch Perkins
Lucy Maud Montgomery
Luther Benson
Lydia Miller Middleton
Lyndon Orr
M. Corvus
M. H. Adams
Margaret E. Sangster
Margret Howth
Margaret Vandercook
Margaret W. Hungerford
Margret Penrose
Maria Edgeworth
Maria Thompson Daviess
Mariano Azuela
Marion Polk Angellotti
Mark Overton
Mark Twain
Mary Austin
Mary Catherine Crowley
Mary Cole
Mary Hastings Bradley
Mary Roberts Rinehart
Mary Rowlandson
M. Wollstonecraft Shelley
Maud Lindsay
Max Beerbohm
Myra Kelly
Nathaniel Hawthrone
Nicolo Machiavelli
O. F. Walton
Oscar Wilde
Owen Johnson
P.G. Wodehouse
Paul and Mabel Thorne

Paul G. Tomlinson
Paul Severing
Percy Brebner
Percy Keese Fitzhugh
Peter B. Kyne
Plato
Quincy Allen
R. Derby Holmes
R. L. Stevenson
R. S. Ball
Rabindranath Tagore
Rahul Alvares
Ralph Bonehill
Ralph Henry Barbour
Ralph Victor
Ralph Waldo Emmerson
Rene Descartes
Ray Cummings
Rex Beach
Rex E. Beach
Richard Harding Davis
Richard Jefferies
Richard Le Gallienne
Robert Barr
Robert Frost
Robert Gordon Anderson
Robert L. Drake
Robert Lansing
Robert Lynd
Robert Michael Ballantyne
Robert W. Chambers
Rosa Nouchette Carey
Rudyard Kipling
Saint Augustine
Samuel B. Allison
Samuel Hopkins Adams
Sarah Bernhardt
Sarah C. Hallowell
Selma Lagerlof
Sherwood Anderson
Sigmund Freud
Standish O'Grady
Stanley Weyman
Stella Benson
Stella M. Francis
Stephen Crane
Stewart Edward White
Stijn Streuvels
Swami Abhedananda
Swami Parmananda
T. S. Ackland

T. S. Arthur
The Princess Der Ling
Thomas A. Janvier
Thomas A Kempis
Thomas Anderton
Thomas Bailey Aldrich
Thomas Bulfinch
Thomas De Quincey
Thomas Dixon
Thomas H. Huxley
Thomas Hardy
Thomas More
Thornton W. Burgess
U. S. Grant
Upton Sinclair
Valentine Williams
Various Authors
Vaughan Kester
Victor Appleton
Victor G. Durham
Victoria Cross
Virginia Woolf
Wadsworth Camp
Walter Camp
Walter Scott
Washington Irving
Wilbur Lawton
Wilkie Collins
Willa Cather
Willard F. Baker
William Dean Howells
William le Queux
W. Makepeace Thackeray
William W. Walter
William Shakespeare
Winston Churchill
Yei Theodora Ozaki
Yogi Ramacharaka
Young E. Allison
Zane Grey